FACING BEREAVEMENT

FACING BEREAVEMENT

Edited by Ann Warren

HIGHLAND BOOKS

Printed in Great Britain for
HIGHLAND BOOKS
Broadway House, The Broadway,
Crowborough, East Sussex TN6 1BY
by Richard Clay Ltd., Bungay, Suffolk.
Typeset by CST, Eastbourne.

Contents

FOREWORD

Each one of us contributing to this book has experienced the death of someone very close to us: a much loved husband or wife; a child—a tiny long-awaited baby, a beautiful little daughter, or a son on the verge of manhood; parents—young or older; a close friend—by suicide.

In the writing of this book, all of us have shed many tears. Probably we had no idea how difficult our particular chapter would be to write, or how many memories, whether recent or long past, would yet again bring us to breaking point.

But many of the writers, in letters accompanying their completed manuscripts, spoke of healing in the remembering, and of tears that had needed to be shed—as if reopening those painful doors had achieved some kind of catharsis: something that all of us needed to re-experience.

Not that the deep scars of bereavement ever really disappear. We have all in turn pronounced the concept that 'time heals' to be a myth—little more than a comforting thought for those who seek to comfort us. Time distances, but the pain goes on, and it can hit us, time and again, at moments when we least expect it to.

Most of all we need our friends and loved ones to bear with us through the pain, to listen and to suffer with us if need be. Sadly for many Westerners this seems a very difficult thing to do. They would rather push the painful memories away out of sight, covering them with a neat little verse—and praying that they will go away for good! In this way, they will not have to face our terrible grief or to hear the anger and the soul-searching that they would much rather not know about.

I have never forgotten the words of a young widow who had once been a believing Christian but had lost her faith through the total inability of others in the church to come alongside and feel the pain with her. They had given her Bible texts and 'good books' to read—but they couldn't, or wouldn't, suffer with her, as Christ himself has commanded us to do. Eventually, as she apparently did not quickly 'recover' in the way that they expected her to do, they implied that her faith was not what it should be—and, one by one, left her to cope on her own. Not surprisingly this girl, who had so recently lost the man she loved most in all the world, soon lost her faith as well. If this was the only kind of love that believing Christians could show, she, not unnaturally, began to question the kind of God they believed in.

So often we gloss over the subject of death and bereavement, only returning to this when we feel safe to talk about it in sufficiently distant and spiritual words—but this is of little help to those at present going through the valley of the shadow of death, who may well be confused by their own bitter thoughts, and hurt by other people's lack of understanding or willingness to listen.

In the fast-moving plastic world of the twentieth century, where death and bereavement are an uncomfortable reminder of our fragile mortality, this whole subject has been removed to the safety and distance of a clinical hospital ward and a brief notice in the paper. In place of the Victorian death bed scene, with all the family gathered round to pay their last respects, and to see that death, that 'last enemy', was not, perhaps, quite so terrible and fearful as they had imagined, we have total 'shut out'—a condition in which dark and sinister fears breed and multiply.

Few people today have seen someone die, so few have had the experience of seeing the peace that often comes, even at the end of terrible suffering. Few have even seen a dead body, except when cosmetically concealed to create the illusion that nothing has changed—as Evelyn Waugh so cleverly described in his book *The Loved One*.

For such people, death may be nothing but the terrible unknown; but all of us may wonder whether our faith will remain real at death; whether we really will see our loved ones again; whether we can be sure that the promise of eternal life for all who follow Jesus is true.

The last chapter in the book was originally published in booklet form. Entitled 'Dying—the Greatest Adventure of My Life', this remarkable document was written by a young Christian doctor facing terminal cancer, in the full and frightening knowledge of exactly what that would involve for him. He writes: 'Dying makes life suddenly real. Watching my slow physical deterioration reaffirmed my belief that there is something else within which will survive, because, if for no other reason, my personality stayed the same in spite of the eroding bodily form in which it was confined.'

All of us contributing to this book share a common Christian faith, but there is nothing simplistic or superspiritual in what has been written. Neither is there any attempt to conceal the pain or the questioning. The comfort that our faith has given us is mentioned only where this genuinely fits into the picture—and is not in any way contrived. Instructions given to every writer were to say exactly how bereavement felt—and how it still feels.

Some people may find it hard to cope with the anger and the questioning expressed in these pages; others may be amazed at the quality of faith and trust shown by a particular writer or writers. The fact is, we—the writers —are all different and express ourselves in different ways. For this reason, and because those reading this book will also be unique individuals, some chapters will be helpful to some, others to others.

If you are at present struggling to cope with a recent bereavement, or have just been told shattering news about what lies ahead, then my prayer is that somewhere in these pages you will find a glimmer of hope and comfort—or the bright threads of faith far ahead at the end of the valley.

If you are trying to come alongside someone who has been bereaved, I hope you will find much in this book to help you to do so sensitively and positively.

One thing is certain—we all have to face death and bereavement at some time in our lives.

Ann Warren

1   **Just Another Baby**   *Jim Smith*

The Rev Jim Smith is an evangelist with the Church Pastoral Aid Society and has a special concern for evangelism among men. He has written books which reflect this interest: *Manhunt, The Christian Man* and *Questions Men Ask* (Kingsway).

He was chairman for counselling and follow-up for Mission England in the north-east, and was involved in youth training and outreach.

He is married to Mary, and they have four sons.

Mary and I have been married for seventeen years and have four children—David (15), John (13), Paul (6) and Stephen (2). Five years ago, when I was the Vicar of two former mining villages in the north-east of England, another son was born to us, but he was very premature, and lived for only three hours.

The notes I kept of what happened to us, from the time of Philip's conception to his first anniversary, form the basis of what is written here. I have tried to tell the story exactly as it happened, with all its confusions, in the hope that other parents following in our footsteps will be encouraged.

When Philip died, we found that we had become members of a very large group of grieving parents who are largely forgotten by family and friends. Relatives understand grief for the death of a child, but find it very hard to understand why we are so hurt at the death of an infant who lived for only a few hours. As far as they are concerned, such babies never achieve the status of 'people' and are therefore forgotten. But for their parents, these tiny human beings are in every way real people—our own children—and we grieve for them with all our hearts.

So here is our story written on behalf of the thousands and thousands of parents who have lost babies. We hope that it will help others to understand better.

Every pregnancy of Mary's has come as something of a surprise to us. All our precautions seem ineffective. When we went on holiday five years ago, Mary was expecting yet again. We didn't tell our children, as we were waiting for the results of a test from our local surgery.

When we rang up from the depths of Norfolk and asked for the result, the receptionist, whom we knew well, started to giggle. When she told Mary that the result was positive, we were thrilled, but Mary had to be sure.

'Are you certain you've got the right Mary Smith?' was her query. More laughter from the surgery, and that settled it.

When we told the boys, they were delighted. David rolled over and over on the floor, kicking his legs in the air. It was a lovely family moment. My parents politely enquired if we ever planned to stop having children, and I wondered how I would get four in the car. We joked about having to buy a bus, and hire the local café for our family meals.

Mary has always had some difficulties during pregnancy, and we were soon put in touch with the hospital. On our very first visit the consultant voiced his concern.

Mary's IUD coil was still in place and this, he warned, could give rise to complications. Not long afterwards, Mary began to leak fluid from the womb, and had to go into hospital for the first of many short stays. The leaking fluid worried us of course, but we got used to it happening and, each time, things cleared up quickly. After a while, however, I began to reflect on what the consultant had said. Mary was blooming, and was quite certain that everything would be all right, but other women in the same ward with the same problem were losing their babies. Uneasily I started to wonder quite what lay ahead of us.

By the middle of the summer, we were no longer the excited and happy family we had been in Norfolk. The frequent stays in hospital were causing a great deal of anxiety for both of us. Mary had to lie quietly in bed, and this gave her too much time to think and worry.

I tried to keep the older children going in their usual routine, as well as spending more time with Paul, so that he wouldn't feel the absence of Mum too much. At the same time, I was carrying on with my job as well as keeping Mary cheerful.

During this period, I came to understand why housewives get so tired. I also experienced the loneliness of a father in this position. People were very concerned about Mary, and rightly so. But I was getting more and more behind with things, and could have done with some comfort myself.

By the middle of the summer we both needed a break from it all, so we booked a holiday in a very quiet part of Scotland. A few days before we were due to leave, Mary was back in hospital again. Fortunately she was soon out and, with the doctor's guarded encouragement, we went away. I did all I could to keep Mary rested, and we had a few days' relaxation, but then she had a massive leak, and we rushed home, then went straight to the hospital.

This time the consultant told us that she would have to stay until the baby was born in another three months. I was booked to work away from home for a fortnight, so the children stayed with my parents, while I went off to work. During that fortnight, I put so much money into the local call box that I felt I had bought the thing!

On the day I was due to return, Mary had a haemorrhage, and the hospital advised me to come home at once. I went straight to the ward and found that Mary had gone into labour. Her blood pressure was dangerously high, so no attempt was going to be made to delay the birth even though the baby would be premature. I settled down beside her, tired and afraid, to watch the night out. It seems an odd thing to remember, but that night I read the whole of the book *All Quiet on the Western Front* and then got a little sleep. Shortly before 6.00 a.m., I woke with a start, knowing in my heart that the crisis had come.

We were quickly moved to the delivery room. Surrounded by technology and much loving skill, two very frightened people wondered what the next minutes would bring.

Philip was born just after 6 a.m. I could tell immediately from the faces of the staff that all was far from well. They put him into an incubator, to transfer him to the special care unit, but first they showed him to us. We were afraid to look, although I don't know why. We never touched him, and we deeply regret this missed opportunity. We were never able to communicate with this tiny life, to tell him that, despite all the pain and all the struggle, we loved him, and that he would always have a place with us.

In the special care unit, the staff did all they could, but when the consultant came to see me a little later, he said, 'I'm so sorry. He's so weak. If only he can last a few hours then perhaps . . .'

With Mary sleeping in her room, and Philip in the special care unit, I came home for a wash and some food. Just before 9 a.m., the phone rang. It was a sister from the hospital, whom we had got to know well. I can hear her voice now. She just said, 'Mr Smith, oh Mr Smith . . .' But I knew what had happened.

'It's OK sister,' I said. 'I understand. I'll be right back.'

I've never forgotten that moment, and I never will. It is burnt into my memory. I was overwhelmed with sorrow and anger, despair and loneliness. In an instant, my life was changed. I sighed a very deep sigh, and drove back to the hospital.

I could hear Mary crying long before I got to her room. One of the staff was holding her, she was crying, too. I took Mary in my arms, and she sobbed, 'My baby, oh my baby.'

I couldn't think of a single thing to say.

There were things that had to be done. Mary needed sleep and rest to regain her physical strength and begin to come to terms with what had happened. I had to make the practical arrangements for Philip's funeral.

I went to register his death and was a little shaken to be told, as gently as possible, that first I would have to register his birth. When I thought about it, I realised that this would have been necessary, but at the time, grief stricken, I found this hard to accept. I arranged the funeral, and conducted it myself in the crematorium. Mary was too ill to leave hospital, so just one friend came with me. It was strange to be marking the end of a life which I had helped create, but right nonetheless.

Apart from this necessary task, nothing else was important to the two of us. All the things that we had valued before, seemed worthless in the light of this personal tragedy. We thought of a holiday, and were getting round to fixing one, when we realised that we were only running away from reality. So we came home, to face whatever lay ahead.

While Mary was in hospital, she only had to face me, but I had to face the world. I felt that if I heard the words, 'I'm sorry,' again, I would scream. On the first Sunday morning after Philip died, every member of my congregation said it to me. Of course I would have been hurt if they hadn't, but all the same I wished that I could have been spared this, if only for a few weeks. At least, eventually, I got used to having this said to me, so that when Mary was faced with the same thing, I could help her through.

When the children returned home, I told them exactly what had happened. I said that Philip had been born, but he had not been strong enough to live, and now he was dead. They were very upset, but there was little I could do to console them at that moment.

My parents stayed for a while, but we were glad when they went home. It wasn't that we didn't love them, or appreciate their help, but we needed to set about picking up the pieces on our own, as a family. As we looked at the empty cot and the empty pram, and faced the emptiness of our own lives, we knew that, however hard we tried, things would never be the same again.

Mary didn't want to go anywhere, or speak to anyone. Physically she still had to recover from Philip's birth, and emotionally her spirit was crushed. The only way to get her out was to go with her, and so we went everywhere together. At first she would cross the road to avoid meeting people, but slowly she became able to talk to them.

We went out for a number of restaurant meals; in these more impersonal settings, she began to relax and to talk about what had happened. Many people wanted to visit, but we took a firm line. Mary wasn't well, and couldn't cope with long visits, so we kept them short and few. The children were a great help to us. Their lives had to go on, and Paul, who was very young, kept bouncing around, being himself, and forcing us back into the real world.

Many of the things people did and said were of little help to us, as we tried to rebuild our lives. This is a hard thing to say, especially as they were only trying to help. Flowers and cards poured in to our home, but a house full of flowers only served to remind us that the house was empty of baby.

Most of the cards were unsuitable. Many of the words printed in them were along the lines of, 'He's happy with

Jesus.' The letters could also be difficult. We didn't need holy thoughts, or sermons about the love of God. Perhaps I'm being a bit hard, but this was the effect that the flowers, cards and letters had on us at the time. One card *did* comfort us. It was from a couple who had lost a baby a year before us. They said: 'We know what you are going through, and we know you'll be strong.'

Some comments hurt us a lot, although they were said from the best of motives; comments such as:

'Philip is better off where he is.'

'At least you didn't have him long.'

'You're young—you can try again.'

'You've got a lovely family already.'

'Three's enough.'

I often thought that if people were to stop to think what they were saying, they would keep silent. But most people just don't know what to say, and so fall back on platitudes. This applied to some of our family and friends, as well as to some of the doctors, nurses, consultants and ministers whom we met. It seemed that, regardless of background, some people lacked understanding of our pain.

The hardest comment of all was, 'God has taken him.' Mary and I are both committed Christians, and much prayer had gone into our pregnancy. We were finding it hard to understand how God, whom we loved so much, had allowed this to happen to us. Mary was doing much better than I was. I will quote exactly what she said: 'I knew that God was still with me. Jim was very bitter, but I couldn't be. Throughout all the upheavals of pregnancy I had known God's presence with me many times. Even though we had lost Philip, I couldn't forget all that God had done for me. I knew his love and compassion, and I learnt to turn moments of despair into moments of prayer.'

Personally, I was finding it much harder to hold on to

my faith. I thought that God had let me down, and I felt that I could never trust him again. I had a long way to go before I would be able to get my faith together again.

Some visitors were very sensitive but others behaved as if nothing had happened or wanted to know every detail as if they had some right to know our private grief. One health visitor was particularly insensitive. She sat down, and said, 'I know that you've lost a baby recently. How did it happen?' We didn't tell her, and I asked her to leave.

We recognised at the time that visitors couldn't win. If they didn't ask us about Philip, we thought they didn't care, but if they did ask us, we felt they were prying. Such confusion is all part of grieving which is a very complicated process. There are many emotions involved and we are not always able to control them. One night, when I was feeling particularly low, I listed the many different feelings raging inside me. These were: sadness, helplessness, emptiness, pointlessness, anger, hostility, bewilderment, frustration, lostness, valuelessness. We were certainly a hurt and confused family.

Other people's babies were causing us a lot of sorrow too. Every time we saw a baby, we thought of Philip. Every full pram reminded us of our empty one. A few months after Philip had died, I conducted a baptism service in my church. As I held the beautiful baby, I could see that Mary was crying, and so was another mum who had lost a baby just before us. Such feelings stayed with us for a long time. After a year, we were thinking that Philip would have been one, and then we would look at other one year olds, and realise the absence of ours. A few months after Philip had died, friends came to tell us that they were expecting their first child, adding, 'We didn't tell you sooner—we weren't sure how you would react.'

Progress was very slow. For every move forward,

there seemed to be at least half a move backwards. Some days were good, and we could face all sorts of things. Then suddenly the blackness and pain would close in and we would feel that there was no hope for us. Anything could trigger off despair—a thought, a pram, a photo, a remark. This was very confusing for our friends. Often, after agreeing to go out, when the time came, one or other of us would feel dreadful and so we would both stay at home.

Mary and I talked and talked, night after night. We had only 180 minutes of life to remember, and we didn't want to lose a single second of it. Mary cried a lot, but I couldn't cry. On the morning that Philip died, on my way home from the hospital I saw some children playing, and my eyes misted over. I should have stopped the car, and cried my heart out then and there. Foolishly I didn't, and after that I found that the tears and all my emotions were trapped inside me. I kept going somehow, trying to hold the family together and to keep working but I paid a very high price for the mistake of responding in this way.

There were painful decisions to make. The carrycot and the pram couldn't stay in the house for ever, and the baby clothes couldn't stay on the spare bed. After five months, Mary let me put the carrycot away. When the pram went, I comforted her by saying, 'Darling, if we need another pram, we can always buy one.' The baby clothes we gave away to an expectant mum. I took them to her one day when Mary was out shopping. We both agreed that this was a sensible use of the things, but I had to do it. I suspected at that time that one or two little garments had been hidden away in the house, and I subsequently found this to be true.

One most positive thing at this time was that Mary got a part-time teaching job. This gave an order and a purpose to her life, which she desperately needed. She had to get up, because she was expected at work. She had to mix with other people, and this helped to change her inward-looking attitude. The job was definitely one of the keys to the healing process that was beginning in her life.

The first Christmas after Philip died was a very bad time for us. The carols, the tinsel, the advertisements for toys and the Christmas lights in the streets all made us feel our loss most acutely. Christmas is traditionally a happy time, but for millions it is a time of sharpened grief, as we were now learning.

Later Mary said, 'As Christmas came near, the sadness got worse and worse. I had to write down every detail, so that I wouldn't forget anything. Holding on was my one aim. Even though I wrote and wrote, it didn't bring any lasting satisfaction. So I burnt what I had written—as a kind of ceremonial act.

'Jim told me that I had to let go of the memories. They were like a lead weight round the neck of a drowning man. I knew that I had a choice to make. I could either make a new beginning, or let myself be destroyed by the past. I decided to let go and make that new beginning. It was a turning point in my experience.'

We did our best for the sake of the other children but we were glad when Christmas day was over, and even happier when all the decorations were put away. As we entered the new year, we felt that we had turned a corner of some kind. Much darkness lay ahead, but we were also catching glimpses of the light.

I was beginning to put my own faith back together. I realised that it was not a question of whether I would suffer or not—that had already been decided. My choice was whether to suffer with or without God. I decided that I was better off with God, and this decision began to bring me peace again.

But I still couldn't cry. I had to wait awhile for tears. They started to flow in Jerusalem. A friend, seeing the exhaustion of the family, had sent us to Israel for a week and, in one of the holy places, I was able, for the first time, actually to thank God for Philip. When I got back to my hotel room, three large tears, one after another, welled up in each eye, rolled down my face, and dripped on to my hand. These tear-drops weren't much, but they were a beginning: the first of many that would flow in the months to come.

Our whole family was grieving. Initially, to some extent, Mary and I overlooked the children's needs, but we were stopped in our tracks by remarks such as:

'Daddy, when I go to bed and think about Philip, I'm really sad.'

'Daddy, I'm really sad, because when I get to heaven Philip won't know me.'

'Daddy, don't forget to pray for Philip.'

After this, we tried to include the children in our grief, which seemed to be the right approach, and to recognise and share theirs.

By the Spring, most people thought we were back to normal and, in one sense, we were, but we were not prepared to forget Philip; besides, all kinds of things reminded us of him and, in some cases, knocked us back.

One day Mary said, 'You know, when I was expecting Philip, I hung some wallpaper, if only I hadn't . . .' We were for ever walking into the 'if only' trap. I would tell her not to be so silly, and then catch myself thinking, 'If only I had done more for Mary when she was expecting.' We were working out our sorrow, of course, but we needed to try to resist the temptation to blame ourselves for what had happened. This would have been pointless: what had been done couldn't be undone; and we had to move ahead, not back.

Slowly we grew through the grief, becoming more sensitive and caring people and closer as a family.

Philip's first birthday was the last great trial for us. We

had no idea beforehand how bad it would be. It was as though we had made no progress at all since the time we had been in the delivery room, with all the fear and horror; as though all our confidence had evaporated. No words can describe the dreadfulness of that day. It was like Philip's death all over again. But in a strange way it was very helpful too. We were forced to examine the memories which we had been trying to hide. Afterwards, they were never quite so painful again.

I was as painfully aware of the anniversary of Philip's funeral as I had been of the anniversary of his death. On that first anniversary, I had to conduct a funeral service in the same place and on the same morning as I had conducted Philip's funeral service. I thought I would burst into tears; instead, when I saw the grief of the family, I realised that I was in the best possible position to help them.

We are a fairly normal family. Yet we found the death of our tiny son shattering beyond belief. We never imagined that one life, and that so short, could have such an impact. I suppose things were made worse by feeling that few understood our plight or our pain. Philip was just a new born baby, and to many, he was just another infant mortality, quickly forgotten. Yet he was never that to us. He was, and still is, very much a part of our family. When we are asked how many children we have, we say four because it causes less embarrassment. But in fact we have five children—four here and one in heaven. We will never forget Philip; and Stephen, who arrived after him, will never replace him. There only ever was, and only ever can be, one Philip. Human life is precious, and we value this child, as we do all our children.

Through our time of trial, we have learnt some lessons, which we would like to share briefly, as an encouragement to other parents following the same path, who might be wondering whether there can ever be an end to their sorrow.

We have learnt that grief is hell on earth; in particular, grief for an infant towards whom one has been unable to show love, brings sorrow that almost defies description.

We feel that we have become better people through our grief. We are more understanding of the hurts of others, and more able to share their pain. We believe that this has made us more useful to our fellow human beings.

Philip's death has helped us to see the difference between the valuable and the worthless. We no longer place much value on money, cars, homes, status and position. When weighted against one human life, these are worthless.

Our greatest lesson was in what we learnt about God. Mary and I both believe in Jesus Christ. I've known him since I was three, and Mary since just after we were married. Our faith was tried to the limit through Philip's death. Mary had the best grasp of things, but by the grace of God, we have both emerged stronger in our faith. We don't know why Philip died, or why God didn't answer our prayers for his life. But we're coming to realise that God only ever wants the best for us, and that somehow this *is* the best, although we don't know why at the moment.

We've learnt that God doesn't stand outside our lives, watching us struggle with a list of rules, but that he comes right in, right into the delivery room, or wherever we are, to share our sorrow with us. We're wholeheartedly grateful to him. We don't know how those without faith manage to survive.

Philip died on 31st August 1981. On Christmas day, 1983, at morning service, Mary was crying at the memories and emptiness of it all. Unknown to us, God had already devised one answer to our needs and, on August

20th, Stephen John was born. At this moment he is terrorising the plants in the garden as his brothers did before him. I'm sure Philip would have done the same.

'What a Beautiful   *Rosalind Allan*
       Little Girl That Is!'

Rosalind Allan, her husband and children now live in a household of nine, including the family who have come to share her work with the Good News Trust. The story of how this came about and of her adventures in the Stamford Good News van is told in *Out of the Ark* (Hodders). The van was the first of what is now a nation-wide network of free travelling libraries, lending books to many homes.

An English teacher by profession, Rosalind has an interest in literature which, since her renewal in the Holy Spirit, has assumed a new perspective. Sharing Christian books has brought improbable and exciting experiences, from learning about goat-rearing and breadmaking in a farm kitchen, to attempting to ease the spiritual anguish of a newly converted murderer in a prison waiting room.

In this chapter she tells of the sudden loss of her first child Penelope. Rosalind and Hugh Allan's other children are now teenagers. Juliet, the oldest, was too young to remember what was happening around her at the time of Penelope's death but memories of that event, eighteen years on, still wring her mother's heart. However, if Penelope had not died, Rosalind's life would not have been turned upside-down so positively by the Lord. Death, in this case, certainly brought newness of life.

When I first realised that the London taxi ferrying my husband and me through the streets around St. Pancras was nosing its way to the office of the Registrar, not this time of Births, but of Deaths, I was appalled that the rest of the world had not stopped. I was on an incredible film-set of which no one else seemed aware.

If you have been through a similar experience yourself, you may recognize the feeling of detachment from reality and of being apparently alone.

'Spina bifida is a division of the spine. It is congenital . . . and can be accompanied by a hydrocephalic condition . . . Cerebral palsy is caused by damage to the child at birth . . . uncontrollable spasms of the muscles . . . no known remedy . . . blind from birth . . . deaf from birth . . . mongoloid . . .'

Such thoughts raced through my mind as I lay waiting for another contraction. Teaching in a school for physically handicapped children at the time of conceiving my first child, had given me far too much half-information. The teenagers I had grown to know and love were, many of them, maimed from birth. There was nothing one could do, it seemed, to prevent such misadventure, and no one could predict the birth of a grotesquely mal-formed baby. My thoughts muzzed into weary sleep.

Waiting, all waiting.

Then, suddenly, all was action.

'Three whole days! It's quite long enough for the first confinement,' declared the midwife as she bustled into my bedroom. 'Off you go to hospital. It's safer there. Even now you're not likely to deliver for another twelve hours.'

Around midnight, at the end of the fourth day, a surgeon arrived at my hospital bedside and announced the necessity for an emergency caesarean operation. Whoever was in me, was not likely to survive, and nor was I, unless action was taken. The pain was continuing relentlessly and I felt utterly drained.

'*Please* hurry,' I pleaded. There was a flurry of activity which seemed to last hours, but at last I was trundled into theatre where an anaesthetist leant over my face.

'You're away now,' he murmured gently.

It was dark. Hugh, my husband, was beside me. But he was, unaccountably, not alongside me as usual in bed. Wherever was I? I forced open an enquiring eye and looked straight into Hugh's face, bent over mine.

'Thank you for our little girl,' he whispered.

'What little girl?' I asked, bewildered.

'She's in a cot, in with the other newborn babies. You'll see her in the morning.'

I realised suddenly why there was a rustle of plastic under my sheet, why the bed was so narrow, why there was this terrible, heavy, raw feeling across my stomach.

'Is she all right?' I mumbled.

'Yes, ten fingers, ten toes. Perfect!' chuckled Hugh. 'We did agree to Penelope Jane, didn't we?'

I nodded, swallowed and smiled. He was a father, I a mother; we were a family. All was very well at last. While I was trying to take in these facts, Hugh hugged me and left, all too soon. Blearily I looked around the crowded ward where I lay. An Irish voice whispered hoarsely across from another bed, 'You awake? You should have your baby christened, you know. I am, to-morrow. Safest. Might die. Who knows?'

I smiled and withdrew into a haze of plans for our brand new baby. Die? Of course, she wouldn't! We'd wait for a few months and then have a big christening party. The ancestral hand-made gown could come into use again . . . Friends and relatives would celebrate. My nieces and nephews now had a cousin . . . I slept.

Penelope was indeed 'perfect', as far as anyone could tell. No one knew why she had taken so long in arriving, although a nurse suggested casually that it was possible that the umbilical cord had been wrapped around her neck. I was not particularly interested, glad only that my own darling was so beautifully formed and, apparently, whole. Not only had she none of the disabilities I feared, but she was also an exceptionally beautiful child, with black curls, blue eyes, rosy complexion, and, as she grew, an infectious enthusiasm for life, combined with a formidable will. Exceptionally special, as is every child loved by its mother! The christening gown came into its own, just before Penelope was ready to burst out of it.

Soon after the christening, happy and full of adventure, we set sail in the Queen Elizabeth for America, where Hugh was to teach. I wondered vaguely what sort of person Penelope would grow up to be.

We stayed in Washington for two years. One day, towards the end of that time, our sturdy little girl suddenly caused concern. In the morning, Penelope did not wake in her usual bouncy way. I hauled her out from under the mosquito net and offered her her usual cup of rosehip. She flopped against me in a desultory way, her right hand jerking uncontrollably.

Telephone consultations with our family doctor resulted in a very swift ride in his car, lights flashing and siren wailing, to D.C. Children's Hospital. I was impressed that all the traffic should stop for our child to pass. After a shot of phenobarbitone, she gradually came round and was her usual self, fascinated to be in a real hospital where there was a child who was genuinely sick in an adjacent cot. She tried as usual to make friends and to offer her toys, but was whirled almost as swiftly away from me and from the ward for more tests; all proved negative.

'The child appears to be sensitive, very intelligent and quite healthy at the moment . . .' remarked the puzzled neurologist. 'All the same, you must take her to a neurologist on your return to Britain.'

'Just imagine!' I carolled down the phone to my closest friend. 'They tested her for polio, meningitis, *everything!* She even had a spinal tap to make sure she hadn't got a brain tumour. Brain tumour, of all things. No sign—not a thing,' I declared, relieved.

'Uh, huh! . . .' was my friend's non-committal response.

Back in England, November 5th was a new adventure. The evening spun along in a sparkle of fun. But when I crept in at night to tuck in Penelope's blankets, she was having another convulsion. An ambulance sped her to the local hospital, where exactly the same series of tests was set in motion, including the agonizing 'spinal tap', when a needle is inserted into the spine in order to draw off some of the spinal fluid. As before, despite electro-encephalograms and innumerable blood tests, nothing was discovered.

The American doctors had associated Penelope's convulsions with her intelligent sensitivity over the recent shooting of Martin Luther King; their British equivalents blamed Guy Fawkes! I was baffled but very uneasy.

She recovered just as swiftly as she had at first, grew

tall, sturdy and very cheerful, learned to recognize about forty of her favourite words and longed to be old enough to make some British friends at playschool.

On the Sunday before the great day for playschool arrived, Penelope came with us and her recently born sister, Juliet, to church. We sat in our usual pew; the one that gave swiftest access to the door and the freedom of a country churchyard. However, on this occasion Juliet was the big distraction. Juliet 'needed' to learn to put her thumb in her mouth and go to sleep. Penelope lay down in the aisle beside her, curled up cosily in her winter overcoat, thumb in mouth, demonstrating. We were merely embarrassed when, during the ensuing hymn, led loudly by the vicar, she called out to him, over her upside-down hymn book, 'Tops it. You're shouting!'

We were more disconcerted when, during a bracing plod led by Hugh in the January drizzle of the afternoon, a pale-faced child in a red cape lagged far behind, calling in a small voice, 'Carry me, Daddy! I want to be carried home.'

'You're a big girl, now. Two and three quarters and in big red boots. No one's carrying a sturdy girl like you. Look! There's a bulldozer . . .' encouraged Hugh.

Dozer . . . lullabies . . . 'Rock-a-bye bulldozer,' hummed Penelope helpfully. We were glad to get home before the winter drew in upon us more miserably.

Monday was playschool day. Penelope was up early and chose her prettiest dress. But breakfast was a non-event.

'I've got a head-hurts,' she remarked, puzzled. 'I don't want cornflakes. I want to go back to bed.' Upstairs she went. Five minutes later she returned. 'All better now. Now playschool!' But I found her two minutes afterwards curled up on the settee.

'I've got a big, big head-hurts. There!' She pointed to her left forehead.

At last there was a hint of what might be causing the convulsions. The dread which had been with me since the events of November 5th suddenly increased, but at the same time I felt relief that now I could do something positive about it. I telephoned the specialist who had seen Penelope after fireworks night.

'He doesn't come here today,' answered the first hospital. 'He's probably visiting the wards at his other hospitals . . .' Each one I telephoned gave the same reply, until eventually I was advised to track him down at his private clinic. By the end of the morning, I had tracked him down—at his home. But he discovered that I was a National Health patient, claiming his attention out of turn. I had an appointment in February; until February I must wait. I felt embarrassed that it seemed as if I had been trying to jump the queue, mortified that I had now assumed the role of an over-anxious Mum, but above all frustrated to the border of panic at the delay.

The headache grew so much worse during the afternoon that Hugh took Penelope to our own doctor. He found absolutely nothing wrong, but suggested she might be jealous of Juliet. Penelope smiled wanly. Exceedingly proud of her very own baby sister, she did not yet understand the word 'jealous'.

Piercing, uncanny screams rent the air all night long, but a return visit to the family doctor merely reaffirmed his earlier comments. By Tuesday afternoon, Penelope was thrashing around, tossing off her blankets and sobbing incoherently. I knew she needed to catch up on missing sleep in order to shake off whatever was causing this agony. The specialist, the doctor and the health visitor visiting that afternoon, had all dismissed my anxieties. Penelope's natural resistance could, I knew, be fortified by sleep. Anxious and frustrated, I spanked a leg that emerged for the umpteenth time from the covers.

'You'll never sleep if you don't stay still!' I scolded.

That was the last exchange I had with my daughter.

By evening she was in a coma, at last being attended to, as an emergency. The ambulance driver who passed by her prostrate body as she lay on a bed, naked and stripped for examination, expressed some of my delight in her, and of my bewilderment at her comatose state: 'What a beautiful little girl that is! Lovely peaches and cream colouring, black curls . . . Not much wrong with her!'

Once he had examined her, the specialist came over to me, embarrassed and evasive.

'I'm afraid things don't look at all good, Mrs. Allan. She has an extensive brain tumour . . . Was it you telephoning me yesterday? Well, I'm sorry, but it's all rather late now . . .'

'You mean she's going to die?' I asked with an icy calm that amazed me as I heard it. Inside I felt unutterable disgust for this man's previous behaviour.

The specialist gulped, nodded and pronounced, 'We can't tell yet . . . I've arranged for her to go to Great Ormond Street Hospital immediately. I'm sorry, Mrs. Allan.'

Perhaps it was not too late. At least she was now being committed into the hands of caring experts. I assumed at first that I would go in the ambulance, but soon realised that would delay matters as Juliet was temporarily with a neighbour and I had to breast-feed her. So, unable to help, I saw my husband and child being driven off at speed, to the accompaniment of screeching sirens and flashing police escort lights.

Back home my mind raced in every direction like some trapped wild animal. I had to do my part for my daughter. But what to do? I thought of all the friends and relations with whom I could normally share the news; all would be asleep. Then I thought of God, a distant God in my thinking at that time. I thought of Jairus and his daughter, but my praying was incoherent, so urgent that it made little sense. Doubt fastened on firmly: 'God is busy with people who really love him. He can't hear incompetent prayer from anyone as half-hearted as you. Anyway, Jairus was for Bible times. You have doctors now.'

Frantically I telephoned Great Ormond Street: 'They are preparing to operate now, Mrs Allan.' I settled cross-legged on the bed, the telephone in the middle of the eiderdown, and battered at the gates of heaven again and again. Each time, a phone call to the hospital seemed more practical. Each phone call was answered calmly; but there was no further news. No one at all, anywhere, could reassure me.

By mid-morning of Wednesday, Juliet in her carrycot and I had arrived at the hospital. Penelope lay as white as her head-bandages, eyes closed. I was horrified and awed at the sight of tubes leading from every orifice of her body.

'Try to call her back,' encouraged the nurse. 'She needs to wake up now, if she can.'

'Pelpe!' I whispered, embarrassed to call her by the homely nickname. 'Penelope! Come on, darling . . .' A bandaged hand reached up for me. Bandaged? Had they done something painful to her hands now? I dared not touch the bandages and the hand fell back.

'Penelope?' I ventured, again. 'Pelpe! It's your Mummy . . .' No response. 'Please heal her!' I yelled silently, half incredulous that I was really in this situation. Then, for an astonishing few minutes I suddenly felt able to argue with God in my thoughts, and to find him closer than ever before.

'I want you to heal her, please. Oh, please. PLEASE.'

'In your English lessons, you're always quoting Browning: "Man's reach should exceed his grasp, or

what's a heaven for?" What *is* heaven, in your understanding?'

'Oh, a place of bliss, I suppose.'

'Bliss. Meaning What?'

'Utter joy, fulfilment, reassurance.'

'Why, then, are you depriving her of that?'

'Because I love her. After all, I am her mother. You
don't know what that's like. I've looked after her all her
life, shielded her from measles, traffic, any hint of unhappiness. There was all that pain at her birth. She's
mine and I want her. *Please* will you heal her. I know
you can. So please do so. I do believe. PLEASE!'

'One moment. *Who* looked after her all her life?
Didn't I look after you both, especially at her birth?
Who made you her mother?'

'You did. But you don't know what this is like for me.
Look at her, lying there swathed in bandages and stuck
with tubes. I can't even cuddle her or take her hand.'

'Who gave you this love, this mother's love? Did I not
create all the mothers that ever lived? Does my love not
surpass all the love I've ever instilled into all those drop-
lets of my vast creation? My love is utterly boundless and
you're holding your daughter back from receiving it with
me now.'

'Well, if you want her now, you must have her. She's
yours, after all.'

Three minutes after that Penelope stopped breathing.
A scurry of nurses and doctors pelted into the room and
I was told to go and feed my baby. Utterly helpless and
numb, in a side-room lined with files and instruments, I
fed Juliet and waited.

'I'm afraid there was nothing we could do. Penelope
has gone now.' The doctor waited for me to digest the
obvious.

'May I say good-bye to her now you have finished?' I
asked.

Her body lay, warm and cuddly, but absolutely white and still. As I kissed her, I was aware of the real little person blithely floating away above me in the region of the ceiling. She was pausing on her cheery way, concerned to see me all alone and distressed by the form on the bed. I was filled with a great yearning to will her back. But it really felt as if God had spoken to me and although everything was finalised, Penelope's life would never finish. I had to stand back and see.

At first my mind would constantly seek some alternative to the situation I was in. Sitting in that taxi, weaving its way to the Registrar's Office, I very much hoped that if we hurried back to the mortuary we would find that the diagnosis had been a mistake, that Penelope was fit and waiting to go home. But events followed inexorably.

We did return to the mortuary, a fairly low-ceilinged room, furnished in dark wood. Penelope's body lay before the altar, her head still swathed, hands folded stiffly together. I bent to kiss the body, and suddenly realised that the chill flesh was merely a thing, a cast-off. Penelope was somewhere else altogether. I drew back, frustrated, only to glance at the carving above the tiny altar. Two great hands reached down to grasp two chubby little fists. Above were the words: 'Is it well with the child?' and underneath the answer: 'Yes, it is very well.'

'So just take that to heart,' came the gentle rebuke within me.

Nevertheless I wanted to do all I could to proclaim that Penelope had existed, and still did so, somewhere. I collected photographs together, frustrated that recent ones were all of Juliet. Every tiny memento and reminiscence went on record.

Meanwhile, self-accusation and guilt ran rife in me.

Surely I could have foreseen this illness? There had been enough warning lights as I looked back. If I had done so, I could have made better attempts to relieve her suffering. As it was, I had done virtually nothing; in fact I had wasted the last afternoon of her conscious existence trying to talk through the problems of a friend who had called in. Above all, I remembered how I had smacked Penelope's leg, and how I had failed to take her bandaged hand. Those self-accusations were to stay unresolved for years.

The Lord had undertaken to look after Penelope with his abundant love; I now began to be aware of his concern for me too. The Sunday after Penelope's death we were again in church, in the same place, slightly behind the entry door. Hugh and I were kneeling before the beginning of the service. I did not look up, but as I knelt there I 'saw' the door swing open. Instead of the grey January weather I expected, I saw brilliant sunshine. Penelope was passing the church door, swinging along on the arm of a tall, athletic eastern man, at whose face I dared not look. But Penelope was wreathed in smiles and looking straight into his face. She glanced momentarily into the church and said, 'That's my Mummy and Daddy in there. Look after them, won't you?' Then she was off and away, skipping along in the morning sun.

This was in such sharp contrast to my own feelings and to the drear of that January morning that I knew it could not be mere wishful thinking, nor some creation of my own utterly bleak imaginings. Penelope must be very actively alive! In my heart I no longer needed to affirm her identity. I knew, and know still, that she exists.

We planned the funeral to be a celebration of Penelope's last birthday on earth, her first in heaven.

'Now thank we all our God . . . who from our mother's arms hath blessed us on our way . . .' was followed by a voluntary laced with, 'Girls and boys come

out to play.' The congregation were invited home to eat
Penelope's favourite treat: a fourpenny ice cream. The
sad company at the crematorium were greeted with,
'This joyful Eastertide,' in defiance of all gloom. It was
as I peeped at the coffin, disappearing beyond silently-
closing curtains, that I was overwhelmed with horror at
the thought of the engulfing flames. Almost immediately, I was reminded that beside Penelope's body in the
coffin was Bear Dee—he who had played 'Who's afraid
of the Big Bad Wolf?'—and was at peace. After all,
Penelope was elsewhere altogether, skipping along with
Jesus.

During the funeral and after it, I became aware of a
completely new dimension of Jesus alive today. A philo-
sophical friend from the States wrote suggesting that
removal of each earthly joy (Penelope, in this case)
brings dependence on God's unique stability; an uncle
edged his way into the funeral party, bearing a large box
of onions, 'to help you cry'; a bowl of a dozen red roses
from Penelope's friends in the States arrived on the
doorstep; best of all, the children from the neighbour-
hood shyly gave us pictures drawn in school and even
asked to play in our garden. All these little offerings of
love proclaimed Jesus alive, through people.

Mysteriously, all this compassion and concern made it
essential for me to forgive those who had so unwittingly
failed me a few days earlier, especially the family doctor
and the specialist. In the face of this appalling death, any
resentment or accusation would only have compounded
the suffering.

I asked, and everyone asked me, why this death had to
be. Penelope's cancer was an example of the way in
which creation has become distorted by evil, part of
which is due to the sin and stubbornness of all mankind.
Even our little quarrels reinforce Satan's hold over the
universe. It was remarkable how Penelope's death

brought all our relationships into a new light. Alienated friends and even our blood relations had to overcome old animosities as they commiserated with one another. It was amazing how the suffering of one little girl could bring people together as allies, united at last in the face of the common enemy, death. I was awed at the realisation that sin is so powerful in this world that all our ridiculous pettinesses could be reconciled only through such unmerited suffering. Somehow we were being warned that we must pull ourselves together, grow up and stop indulging our grievances, if we were to be of any use in the heavenly battle against evil. How tragic that it often takes a catastrophe to cause us to love one another and to relish life as our heavenly Father designed it.

Every so often I was faced with the question, 'If Penelope's body has been burned and you have allowed them to slice up her brain for medical research, whatever is she herself like now?' I had no answer, until one day I was shown another little picture. I was given a worm's-eye view of a flower border. The flowers above me were jostling and tossing in a sun-swept breeze: daffodils, jonquils, narcissi, primroses and tiny violets. Each represented a person, individually designed and beautiful. Then I was aware of the bulb at the base of one of the daffodils. I thought of the glossy sveltness of a bulb in a seed merchant's tray, of how the bulb itself is well designed, its skin delicately toned. Yet it has to be buried in mud, apparently only to rot and fall apart, but really to divide for the trumpeter-daffodil to grow. Both bulb and flower are recognized as daffodil; yet how glorious the flower is in comparison with the bulb. At the moment, we know only each other's earthly bodies; small wonder that when we are changed, it will be 'from glory to glory'. And yet we shall be recognizable.

In the ordinary world I was a sort of leper. People who

knew I was now bereaved crossed the road when they saw me coming, embarrassed and distressed by the fact that they did not know what to say. Others commiserated as best they could, but were offended if I said that I was at peace, knowing Penelope was being loved far better than she could have been by any of us. Yet I knew I had to declare that fact, in the face of all the tears I shed—frequently at night. During the hours from midnight until three I was beset by doubt. Perhaps my toddler was utterly alone, floating around in limbo eternally, her solitude nightmarish. But each time I turned the matter over to Jesus, I remembered her swinging along on his hand—and the wailing emptiness was filled with light.

By day, the tears were recognized as tears of deprivation. All my hopes and dreams of her at school, growing up, having a career, a boyfriend and her beautiful wedding, were shattered. The pain was exacerbated whenever any girl of a similar age reached one of these milestones. I know now that, in a sense, those tears are very selfish.

It was not for some two or three years that the Lord dealt with my recriminations and guilt feelings about my 'last dealings' with Penelope, when I spanked her leg. I was recounting the story to my husband's elderly aunt, Dorothy.

'You had a very happy relationship with her, didn't you? She wasn't old enough to make you unhappy,' she said.

'But, Dorrie, the last thing she knew of me in her life here was that I spanked her leg. How can I ever forgive myself?'

'Ah, but you did it out of love and concern for her. She now fully understands you and herself. From her new perspective in heaven, she'll understand that behaviour and love you for it. Surely you can forgive yourself, if she already has?'

And it was soon after that conversation that I realised that it is Satan who accuses us, on and on; Jesus shows what is wrong only when we can do something about it to put it right. So Satan, the accuser of the brethren, must be disposed of by Jesus.

There are resurgences of horror and frustration for all who lose a child. But through Penelope's loss I have found deeper, greater friendships than I ever had before. There is indeed 'a place somewhere'. There is fresh meaning in that old song when we allow Jesus to 'hold our hand and take us there'. He'll lead us through suffering; but there is a bond, too, among all those whose hearts have been broken.

> *The bread is the Body.*
> *In order to be shared,*
> *The bread must be broken.*
>
> *So life, so grief and breaking;*
> *So giving and sharing and becoming*
> *The Body and the Bread.*

Elizabeth Boot first trained in London as a medical
secretary, worked for three years at Guy's hospital
medical school, and then for two years at Capernwray
Hall as secretary to the principal of the Bible School.

Just before they were married, she and her husband
Tony bought Min-Y-Don, Gwynedd in Wales, to open
this as a Christian Holiday Adventure Centre at Easter
in 1961.

At Min-Y-Don, Elizabeth works officially as the
administrator, but more often than not finds herself acting as Jack of all trades!

All their four children were born 'in Wales' and
brought up at the centre, where they learned to love the
freedom of the outdoor life. It was here that Elizabeth
first learned the tragic news of her only son's death.

The front door slammed and I heard my handsome, fit nineteen-year-old son say, 'Susie, let's go canoeing.' We live on the shores of a tidal estuary, and I looked out of the lounge window at the wildly undulating waters of a full tide, whipped up by a fierce wind, and thought, 'Surely he's not seriously thinking of canoeing in those conditions!' Simultaneously, I knew that he *was* serious; that those were exactly the conditions in which he wanted to canoe; and that this particular sister would rise to the challenge.

For Tim there always had to be an element of risk if he were truly to enjoy the outdoor pursuits for which he was such an enthusiast. He also urgently desired to be first and best at everything he tackled. His three sisters and I were not only daunted but often quite annoyed that he consistently beat us at the competitive sports we all enjoyed. Coupled with this was an innate gentleness and courtesy. He became an expert canoeist and at fifteen was chosen as a member of the Welsh Junior Squad. He never actually canoed for Wales, but did represent his school—St. David's College, Llandudno.

Tim was a keen climber and skier too but when he started training for his Mountain Leadership Certificate he found that in this area he lacked personal discipline. It was a hard lesson for him to learn. I loved climbing with Tim and there were occasions when he and I went off and climbed together. He was always too fast for me, as he was for nearly everyone else he climbed with, until, in the summer of 1985, he matured into a caring leader and instructor and learned to pace himself according to the needs of those for whom he was responsible.

Tony and I own and run a Christian outdoor pursuits centre and our four children survived the rigours of community life. We had two daughters and a son, with approximately two years between each, then an eight year gap before we had another delightful little daughter, Elizabeth. It has been a special privilege to see all of our children commit their lives to the Lord. We tried not to demand more of them than they wanted to give as far as the work in the Centre was concerned, so it was very special to us when our eldest daughter, Jenny, and also our son Tim, volunteered to work for us during the summer of 1985. Both had skills that could be fully utilised. We were glad, too, that Susie, our second daughter, was able to attend the Capernwray Upward Bound Course in Austria that summer. She already had a degree in P.E. and was building up her experience in outdoor pursuits. We looked forward to one or all of them coming into the work with us and taking over at some stage. It was particularly exciting to see the way Tim was accepting responsibility and the enthusiastic way he was developing new and interesting activities on the estate. During the summer of 1985 he relieved his father of much of the burden of organising the outside pursuits. He was also able to share his faith easily and naturally. The way ahead seemed clear and assured. We had a son who was not only increasingly capable, but also willing to take a share and play a leading role in the work at Min-Y-Don.

We were not surprised when, in the Spring of 1985, Tim asked our permission to spend five or six weeks in the autumn climbing with an experienced instructor in the European Alps. It was exactly the experience and opportunity he needed; but we did have some anxiety about this. A little reluctantly we told him to go ahead and make the necessary arrangements. Our worries were only those of any parent with a son or daughter participating in an activity with a high element of risk, but when Tim first put forward the idea I did, fleetingly, have a feeling of impending disaster. I kept this feeling to myself, not even wanting to share it with my husband, and certainly knowing that it would not be right to dissuade Tim on the basis of mere intuition. He assuaged many of our worries when he explained that his instructor was highly trained and experienced in climbing on ice and snow and on heights in excess of 10,000 feet. They were very well equipped, being members of the Austrian Alpine Club, which gave them access to all the Alpine huts, and had sensible plans for climbing routes and periods of rest.

After a very busy year, Tony and I had planned a two-week holiday in Austria. We loved to be in the mountains with time to walk, climb and relax together. Our two eldest daughters were in Austria that autumn for three months, attending the one-term Capernwray Bible School in Schladming. So, for a brief period, five of us were in Austria at the same time. We had left Elizabeth staying with friends in Tywyn so that she didn't have to miss school. Tim had flown out a week after us and he spent a day and night in Mittersill where we were staying. We took him on the cable car up the Hahnenkamm in Kitzbuhel, one of the World Cup Ski runs, and had a lovely morning together before seeing him off on a train back to Innsbruck.

I shall never forget his boundless enthusiasm at the prospect of some 'real climbing' or the hug that he gave me as he said goodbye; and the picture of his jaunty, upright figure, striding off to catch a train in a country he had never visited before, will ever remain with me.

Thankfully, we did not know that this would be the last time we would see our son alive.

Our holiday over, we returned home.

At 2 p.m. on 29th October the phone rang. Tony was alone in the house as I had gone into the nearest town to the bank. The voice with the New Zealand accent of Tim's instructor came over loud and clear saying, 'It's about the accident—Tim is dead.' He had died the previous afternoon as the result of a fall down a ravine which had broken his neck. For twenty-four hours his three sisters, Tony and I had lived, laughed and slept without knowing that his life had been taken. The police officially informed us about twenty-six hours after the accident, but we still had no idea exactly what had happened or when he had died.

I arrived home that afternoon to find a white-faced husband sitting in our kitchen drinking coffee. As soon as I came in through the door he ushered me into the lounge and made me sit down. My immediate thought was that my very elderly mother had had an accident or died. When Tony said, 'Tim is dead,' the shock almost paralysed me. We clung together and for some time I did not react—the shock was too great. Why? When? Where?—These questions hammered away at us but were, at that point, completely unanswered.

As we sat together trying to draw some comfort from each other we both began to realise that there were urgent decisions and phone calls to be made. What distressed us most was the lack of information. We did not know when Tim had died, what exactly had happened, how long he had been left on the mountain or where his body had been taken. The police, the Foreign Office and the British Embassy in Vienna knew nothing. The Consular Office in Innsbruck were eventually able to find out for us that his body was in Innsbruck and that the Austrian police had his personal possessions. Tony had already informed his older brother, David, and Philip Malin (one of the elders in our church); these two dear men undertook the unenviable task of making the news known.

The next urgent task was to contact our two eldest daughters; we were worried that the news might already have gone out on Austrian television. We had no trouble in getting through to the Principal of the Bible School and he and his wife had the girls in their apartment and broke the news to them. Our youngest daughter, Elizabeth, then aged eleven and a half had gone straight to a music lesson from school that afternoon and had to be picked up at 5 p.m. in a village 6 miles south of us— Tony and I having decided that we had to get her home before saying anything to her. How on earth were we going to tell this gentle, affectionate little girl that her hero of a brother had lost his life? I drove down to pick her up. For a brief period I had to behave as if nothing unusual had happened and then break the news to her myself (Tony was busy with the local undertaker when we arrived home). I managed to do this partly because of the state of shock I was in but mostly, I now believe looking back, because God gave me a special anointing of his strength at that time.

Then I felt terribly alone and longed for the presence of a Christian friend—not necessarily to do anything but just to be with us.

Our next concern was my elderly, widowed mother who lives alone in Tywyn, thirteen miles from us. We needed, and succeeded in finding, someone who could go and tell her, and then stay with her for a while. She took the news bravely and calmly as she has always done with so many difficult situations in her life.

On the day that this awful disaster hit us, we were in

the middle of clearing up after one weekend conference and preparing the Centre for a group of fifty due to arrive the very next day. We debated whether to cancel this booking, but it had been made months in advance, and we decided it would be unfair to spoil the holiday these people were all looking forward to. God honoured this decision, as this group from a church in Bristol truly enjoyed themselves and were blessed during their time with us, and booked to come again in 1986.

However, we badly needed practical help and two of our closest friends, Gerald and Gwen Stevens didn't need to be asked—they just came of their own accord and dealt with the rest of the cleaning and preparation and then stayed to receive the guests and act as front-runners. We contacted another couple, Eric and Chris, who came in every day for the rest of that week. These four not only showed us how much they cared, but also shared in our grief and distress as much as they were able. They lifted an immense burden from our shoulders and shielded us from painful contact with strangers.

That first afternoon and evening the phone rang incessantly; a local policeman arrived with official notification, but no news of what had happened; the undertaker came needing a signature and to have an initial discussion as to how to proceed. In days to come, we were to discover how complicated and difficult the situation was. We had already been put in touch with an international firm of undertakers in London who assured us they could deal with all the formalities in Austria so there was no need for either of us to go out there. Early evening, as soon as her duties had finished at the local hospital, Gwen Stevens arrived and was almost as shocked and distressed as we were. There was little she could do, except make one of the first of the inevitable cups of tea and stay with us for a while. The fact that she came and was willing to sit in silence with us was a great comfort.

In days to come, I often wondered what had happened to our other Christian friends and wished that they would visit. I was shocked when, a week after Tim's death, a member of our church said he felt 'we just needed to be left alone'. How did he know what we felt or needed? As I write this, over twelve months later, I realise that it wasn't that those friends didn't care, but that they felt that they didn't know what to say.

In previous years, that would have been exactly my reaction and I would have felt just as inadequate. My only other close encounter with death had been when my father had died. He had been ailing for some time and had spent the last four months of his life in hospital. My feeling had been one of profound relief when God had taken him to be with himself, although I sorely missed him and realised something of the distress my mother was suffering. But for me, that was nothing like the indescribable agony I went through at the death of one of my own children. I felt as if a large part of me had died—it was like having a major operation with no anaesthetic, being fully aware of all that was being taken away.

The days that followed Tim's death up to his funeral on 9th November, went by in a haze of work, decisions and arrangements. On the day that we had heard the news, we had phoned Tony's eldest sister and her husband, Buz and George Tompkins. Somewhat tentatively we asked if they would come and stay with us for a while as we felt we needed some family support. They immediately dropped all their own family arrangements, and came to stay with us until the day after the funeral. They loved us, cried with us and talked sense when difficult decisions had to be made.

The fact that Tim's death had been the result of a sudden accident outside the United Kingdom resulted in problems that we never expected and which added

greatly to our distress. We received the news that his
body had been flown back to London four days after the
accident and this, in itself, felt like being told all over
again of his death. The local undertaker was allowed to
bring him to the locality and then we assumed that we
could go ahead with funeral arrangements. But the
Home Office stepped in, insisting that all the original
documents should be translated from German into
English (quite a problem in a remote corner of Wales)
and presented to the local coroner. He then ordered a
further autopsy, and another inquest at a later date. The
funeral had therefore to be postponed for several more
days since family and friends were coming from all over
Britain, it was quite a job letting them know of the
change.

For many of you reading this, the details may seem
dramatic, but I pass them on in the hope that, if you are
ever in the position of befriending someone in a similar
situation, you will know something of the trauma involved and not be afraid to go in and help.

The 9th November dawned a grey, cold, blustery day
after a night of heavy rain, and the damp murkiness depressed me still further. I looked out of the bedroom
window, just after 8 o'clock that morning, across the
Estuary, at the mountain that Tim and I had struggled
up together the previous winter on just such a cold, misty
day. I had found it impossible to pray during the previous days, though, paradoxically, had sensed God's
closeness in the sadness that engulfed us, but that morning I asked God to clear away the rain in time for the
funeral. He did more than that. As I looked, a chink
appeared in the clouds and there was a piece of blue sky.
A sign of his promise for that day only—or for the days
and months to come too? The wind dropped, the rain
stopped and the clouds cleared away; and, that afternoon as we set off for the church, a rainbow appeared.

The day had heralded for me an overwhelming feeling of dread and I think the same was true for the four girls (our three daughters and Julie—the girl Tim had come to love); perhaps for Tony too, but he had been kept very busy and this may have made things slightly easier for him. Neither of us had had to carry out the official identification of Tim's body, nor had we seen him since he died, and I hated the thought that I was going to have to come face to face with that cold wooden box that held the body of my son. For days I had eaten very little and been unable to sleep as this dread consumed me. But as God revealed himself in the break in the clouds that morning, there also came an assurance that I need no longer be afraid; and when the hearse arrived at 1.30 that afternoon I felt completely at peace.

We had had difficulty finding a church big enough to hold the funeral service—our own church was too far away and, in any case, was too small—but the caring little community in Arthog heard of this and offered us the use of a chapel in the village, where there would be plenty of space. Sadly, this beautiful chapel is hardly ever used, but a group of local ladies went in and cleaned and polished, and left it sparkling for us. My sister-in-law, Buz, who is very gifted with flowers filled it with the most lovely arrangements—a real expression of her love. We specifically asked that no-one should wear black. As a family we were certain that this service had to be a thanksgiving for Tim's life rather than a mourning over his death. Our close friend Billy Strachan, who led the funeral service stressed this and even evoked a ripple of laughter as he spoke of Tim, the one who always wanted to beat everyone at everything, now having beaten us all into heaven! How Tim would have loved that! He and Billy had always been great friends and, just ten months previously, Tim had dragged Billy up our nearest mountain, Cader Idris, and brought him home again in one piece.

Min-Y-Don was teeming with people all day long. About fifty arrived from all over Britain and were there for lunch. Even more came back for refreshments after the service before setting off again on their long journeys home. Four of the ladies in our church valiantly undertook the catering that day; they simply moved in on us and took over. The busyness and constant coming and going kept us occupied, but when everyone left, late that afternoon, desolation again took over.

The quietness in the house seemed truly 'deathly', and both of us were so restless that we couldn't bear to stay in for long. We sampled nearly every café and restaurant in the area during the next two or three weeks.

We all plunged into a long, very dark tunnel—experiencing this in different ways because God made each of us unique, having differing needs and coping—or not—in different ways. Some months later, our two older girls said that they felt that the grief over the loss of a child that Tony and I were experiencing had to be harder to bear than their grief over the loss of a brother; and that, because of this, they had prayed very particularly for us. When they saw the physical effect that my grief had on me, they must have concluded that God at times was either not listening or else not answering those prayers. I, too, began to wonder where God was; I felt deserted and couldn't understand what was happening to me. I felt ashamed that I was collapsing under the heat of the first really fiery trial that had come my way. I continued to read the Bible but only out of habit. Occasionally a verse would penetrate and I knew God was trying to tell me something, but mostly it was just an academic exercise. I couldn't pray either. What was the point? We had prayed for Tim's safety and apparently God hadn't answered. It was only later that God gave me glimpses of understanding into his perfect ways.

After Tim's death, we had the long haul of winter ahead of us with a spate of 'firsts': the first Christmas after Tim's death, which we didn't feel like celebrating but which we did, in fact, enjoy—having a happy day together as a family; the first New Year, which was worse, because none of us wanted to go into another year without Tim; my birthday, our silver wedding anniversary and Tim's birthday, which all occurred within the space of a few weeks. They couldn't be evaded and they all brought hurt. Tim had loved these special occasions and now he had gone and there was just a great big hole. Also, there was nothing to divert me; hardly anyone phoned or came round. Didn't they care any more, I wondered.

Church became an agony and I fought a losing battle until eventually I stopped going. Was I really expected to praise and worship—there was no energy for either and I just wanted to be still and to have the raging turmoil calmed by God. There was hardly a chorus or a reading that didn't launch some bolt from the blue. I didn't want to hear of other people's problems: I couldn't help them, I had nothing to give. Instead, I needed *their* consolation and reassurance; I needed someone to listen to *me*, hug *me* or just sit and hold *my* hand. Inside I was screaming, 'Lord, I can't handle this; it is destroying me.' But the niggling little answer that kept coming back to me was, 'It won't destroy you, it will strengthen you!'

It must have seemed to some that I was bent on a course of self-destruction. I wasn't getting much sleep, so was constantly tired; and the sight of food usually made me feel ill, so I wasn't eating much and lost a lot of weight far too quickly. It was nice to be slim again, but it got to the stage when even I was a bit shocked at what stared back at me in the mirror. I dragged myself round the Centre trying to do the jobs that I was supposed to do, but there was no joy in it any more. What was the

point of it all? A pain ripped through me every time I
went out of the front door and surveyed the gardens
where Tim had frequently worked, played football or
abseiled down a tree. What was the answer and who
would understand? Was I just neurotic? Ought I to have
quickly risen above this to a life of victory and joy? One
person told me to 'snap out of it'; another said I would
soon feel joyful (which just then I didn't believe); someone else told me to remember I had a husband and three
other children to live for. No doubt it was all well meant
or true, but none of it helped. We are such complex
creatures, our minds and bodies so closely related, so
different in themselves and in their interaction, and we
understand so little of one another. It helped a little
when a friend wrote and quoted Psalm 116 verse 15:
'Precious in the sight of the Lord is the death of his godly
ones.' So the death of God's loved ones *is* of concern to
him and he *does* share our sense of loss: that thought did
filter through to me.

We each experienced grief differently—my grief as
Tim's mother was not the same as my husband's grief as
his father or my daughters' grief as his sisters—and
this gave me a feeling of isolation; also, we were each
dealing with grief in our own way. After the first two or
three weeks, I couldn't even cry with Tony—perhaps we
were both too afraid of causing each other even more
hurt. In time, our heightened awareness of one another's
differing needs drew us into a close bond of love and
concern. At first, for months I felt a sense of guilt at
being unable to give my family the sort of strength and
support they should be getting from me; then I was made
to realise that perhaps, for the first time, *I* was the one
who was in need of *their* nurture and support. I have
never found it easy to show any sort of emotion—prefer-
ring to keep it all tightly under lock and key. As an only
child with elderly parents who frowned on crying, the

showing of anger or the expressing of strong opinions, I became something of a loner, desperately wanting friends but never quite knowing how to relate to others. This reflected in the way I dealt with grief; and all the pent-up emotion and agony became like a tightly curled spring—full of tension and ready to snap at any moment.

In a way that is almost what did happen. Fortunately, a friend persuaded me that there was nothing wrong in seeking medical help, at least with the sleeping problem, and our very understanding GP spent much of his precious time talking to me and offering all the help he could. But the person who really 'turned the taps on' was a friend whom I met at a conference four months after Tim's death. At our first meeting, her gentle sensitivity and understanding began the unwinding of that tightly coiled spring. At last I was able to give myself permission to cry and this, slowly, became a healing experience. Gill invited me into her home to stay, and her friendship and wise counsel taught me to be more aware of the person that is really me and to feel unashamed. This also gave me a better understanding of why I react as I do.

Many believe that grieving is an ongoing process and follows a kind of pattern; I found this to be, in the main, true. In her book *Hour of Gold, Hour of Lead* Anne Lindbergh has said, 'The first days of grief are not the worst . . . One has undergone an amputation . . . still feels the lost limb down to the nerve endings . . . and, while the rebirth is taking place, one is painfully vulnerable. Like gestation [grief] is a slow, dark, wordless process.' I am still so vulnerable and sometimes brittle. Many things hurt and set the fountains flowing—pictures of snowy mountains; advertisements for holidays in Austria; news of the deaths of other young climbers; football results (Tim was an ardent Liverpool fan); Tim's maps and books; his canoe with its competition number still emblazoned . . .

For many, many months I was in the middle of the

tunnel—too far in to see the light from the beginning and not far enough on to see any light at the end. Many times I felt like sitting down in the darkness and giving up the unequal struggle. Two friends in recent months wrote to me and directed my thoughts to that lovely 23rd psalm that most of us learn by heart and then take very little notice of. They both emphasised that the walk had to be *through* the valley of the shadow of death. I couldn't sit down in the deep cold shadow and there was no easy downhill route. I had to go on walking through until I came into the glorious sunshine and climbed to the tops of the hills from which the view could be seen.

Time doesn't heal, but I do believe that God builds a bridge over the deep hole and he teaches us to accept that his will, way and timing are perfect. The grief and deep sense of loss are still with me and I dislike it when people tell me I look better, as if that brings the whole thing to a close. I feel like shouting at them, 'I shall never be better.'

The birth of a baby; the bonding of mother and infant; the fun and worries of childhood and teenage years; the friendship of mother and nearly-adult son—to be followed by sudden and total separation: will I ever be whole again after all that?

Chinks of light are appearing at the end of the tunnel. God is answering prayer in his own time and way.

Again I am drawn to the words of Anne Lindbergh after the death of her young son: 'I do not believe that sheer suffering teaches. If suffering alone taught, all the world would be wise, since everyone suffers. To suffering must be added mourning, understanding, patience, love, openness and the willingness to remain vulnerable.' I agree; and at last I am beginning to believe God's prophecy to his people in Jeremiah 31 verse 13: 'I will turn your mourning into joy, and will comfort you and give you joy for your sorrow.'

4   Overwhelmed by Loss   *Ann Warren*

Ann Warren now lives for most of the year on a small Pacific Island in the North of Papua New Guinea, where her husband eventually found a job after nearly a year out of work—as she described in her last book *Living with Unemployment* (Hodders).

After graduating from St Andrews University, she worked for five years with the BBC in London, as studio manager, scriptwriter and producer, before getting married and going to live for several years in India.

She has worked in a number of different fields since that time—training as pastoral counsellor, serving on the parole review committee of the local prison, on the editorial panel of the Church of England Newspaper and as a member of General Synod of the Church of England. She has also been a regular contributor to the TVS late night television programme 'Company', and has written a number of other books including, most recently, *Today's Christian Woman* (Kingsway) and *Free to be Myself* (Hodders).

Living in Papua New Guinea has brought much of her previous work to an end, but it also allows plenty of time for thinking and writing and an opportunity to see what God is doing on a worldwide canvas.

Something woke me suddenly, even before the dawn had begun to break across the sea below our house. I experienced an inexplicable need to pray for my adoptive mother. We were twelve thousand miles away from home at the time, and I had no possible way of knowing what was going on. But when my friend phoned several hours later to tell me that my mother had died unexpectedly at exactly the time I had been awakened, I realised that God had roused me to watch with her in her time of need.

It had been bad enough to leave her in England when we were forced by the unemployment situation to come and work in Papua New Guinea, but her death at Christmas time when we would love to have been home with her, seemed the very worst that could possibly have happened. Had she needed me at the end? Was it the knowledge that the girls were coming out to join us, when she could not, that had made her finally give up?

For the past few years since my adoptive father's death, and following a stroke that had prevented her getting around, my mother had made no secret of the fact that she wanted to go on to the 'better place' which she knew was waiting for her. She always put a brave face on life, laughing and joking about the multitude of inconveniences and indignities that old people often have to suffer; but privately she told me, more than once, that I was to be happy for her when she had gone.

My thoughts went back to the previous Christmas when we had all been together at the candlelit communion in our local church with my mother at the altar rail in her wheelchair, simply loving every moment of the service. I remembered Gavin Reid commenting in his sermon that it was good to see the Warren family reunited from the far corners of the earth. If only we had been together this Christmas! As it was there was no way that I could even fly home for the funeral.

The flights had been fully booked for months in both directions—and anyway, much as I would have loved to be there, was there really any point? The words of the angel to the women outside the empty tomb came vividly into my mind: 'Why seek ye the living among the dead?' That previous summer she had insisted that if anything like this should ever happen, I was not even to think of coming back. She had greatly valued the time we had had together then, and there would be no point whatsoever once she had gone, she said. At the time I had wished she would drop the whole subject, but now that the worst had actually happened, I was very thankful that I knew for certain she would not have wanted me to go anyway. It was very hard, but part of the price of living and working so far away from home.

All of us have to face up to the loss of parents at some time in our lives, but for me this was yet another tombstone amongst the many that I had already seen erected —another monument to grief. Did my loving heavenly Father realise that I could not have faced another funeral after everything that had gone before? Three months later, as the girls and I stood silently round the small grave that had been dug in the little country churchyard to receive her ashes, while the birds sang in the spring sunshine, I suddenly knew without a shadow of doubt that he had planned it this way all along.

I was only six when my real mother died but memories of that event have remained fresh in my mind, as if it had happened yesterday, rather than many years ago.

I don't think anyone ever explained to me how sick she was; certainly, I never understood this. She was confined to her bed for a long time after my baby brother's birth and then, finally, taken off to a small convent nursing home, just half a mile up the road.

Since the school I attended was right next door, I used to go and visit her every day during break. But as the days went by, I grew more and more frightened and, before long, I really hated the place. My mother was in a very dark room and, for some reason which I could not fully understand, she did not talk to me very much when I went. It appeared that every word was a terrible effort for her, and I suppose I really didn't know what to say or how to cope while I was there. Sometimes the feelings inside me would well up into near panic; even so I still wanted to be with her if she needed me.

Then one day she suddenly asked me if I wouldn't rather stay at school and play with the other children during break, almost as if she had understood all along what I was feeling. She told me not to feel that I always had to come and see her every day. Her words brought the most tremendous sense of release. Not realising the seriousness of her condition, I took my mother at her word the following day.

I remember the joy of being able to stay in the playground that morning, and how wonderful it was to be out in the sun with my friends instead of closeted in the dark silent room where my mother lay.

As the bell rang for the next class, I suddenly noticed one of the sisters from the nursing home talking to the teacher in charge of the playground. Then they both turned to look for me and call me over.

'Where were you today when your mother needed

you?' I was asked reproachfully, and then told, 'She was asking for you just before she died, and we couldn't find you anywhere.'

I will never forget the overwhelming sense of guilt that assailed me. How terrible that I had actually been out enjoying myself whilst my mother had been dying all alone in that horrible dark room! With the unreasoning fear of a small child it seemed to me that somehow her death had been all my fault, hinging on the fact that I had not gone to see her that day. Now there was nothing I could do to put things right; no way of telling her how much I really did love her, or how much I would have wanted to be there with her if I had known that she needed me. This terrible guilt did not leave me for many years afterwards; not until someone prayed with me for the healing of that memory.

I was not allowed to go to my mother's funeral, and for many months it was as if something remained un-finished. My father did eventually take me to see the place where they had buried her, but the whole experi-ence seemed like a hideous waking dream. There was nothing but a mound of freshly dug earth to tell me where my mother was. My father tried to assure me that the stonemasons were already at work carving a marble cross, which would have her name on it and something about how much we loved her. But that anonymous mound of earth only served to underline for me the ugly and unfinished quality of everything surrounding my mother's death.

During the following year things went from bad to worse in my little world. My baby brother, who suffered from Down's syndrome, had been taken into permanent nursing care shortly before my mother's death. I used to go and visit him, but most of the time he didn't know me and it felt as if he no longer belonged to me. The follow-ing year, he died of pneumonia.

Then my father became ill and had to go to hospital at more and more frequent intervals. When he returned, no one seemed to think he looked any better. I loved my father very much, and needed him desperately; but, after my mother's death, he seemed to slip away from me.

A few months later, Edith, our lovely housekeeper, left to get married. Shortly afterwards, my father had to go into hospital yet again. Before he left, he told me to pack up all my things, because when he had gone there would be no one to look after me. I shall remember that evening for the rest of my life.

Without any explanation—because, I imagine, he simply couldn't say the words—he walked me along to the forbidding convent building next door to the school and rang the distant clanking doorbell. Footsteps echoed along the hallway beyond the frosted glass door, and a thin angular nun appeared and almost loomed over me, with her crucifix swinging somewhere around her waist. I think my father tried to explain to me something about having to leave me there, but by this time I was almost paralysed with fright about everything that was happening. I remember that he gave me a brief hug before turning on his heel and almost stumbling down the driveway. He did not even turn round to wave goodbye.

I have often looked back on this moment and wondered what he was feeling and how he coped. For myself, I only wish he had explained more of what was happening. Was it that he couldn't find the words, or did he think I was too young to understand? I felt abandoned, unwanted and deeply afraid.

My mother had been a Roman Catholic and, possibly, he felt that I would be safe and well looked after by the nuns in the convent. I am sure they did their best. But echoing convent walls, endless bells, and figures shrouded in black, however well meaning the people concerned, were hardly the most comforting surroundings for a six year old child.

When our youngest daughter reached that age, many years later, I used to wake up drenched with sweat at the same recurrent nightmare. I could see her sitting all alone in the empty convent dining-room with no one to comfort her; and there was no way that I could reach her, however hard I tried.

The fear reached epidemic proportions, as I began to dread the same thing happening to her in real life. I was practically the same age as my mother had been when she died, and I began to wonder if there really was some terrible kind of threat that hung over our family. I knew that my grandmother had also died when my mother was very young.

As the nightmares persisted, once again I had to look for help in the healing of the associated memories and in the removal of the spirit of fear that had been binding me.

All the same, I saw to it that we made every effort to weave a human safety net for our own children. From a very early age, they were provided with guardians whom they all liked and trusted; and numerous friends promised to come alongside if they were ever needed. Probably they wondered what it was all about, but I honestly think that many parents would do well to make such provision for their own children. None of us knows what any day holds, and I have heard many people, confronted by tragedy, say that they never thought it could happen to them.

I stayed in the convent for what seemed like an eternity, attending the same school next door—but it felt like living on a different planet. Without a welcoming home to return to, and knowing that my father was seriously ill, it was as if I had become another quite different child. I no longer felt a part of the group that I had played with in the past and would often slink off, by myself, to a distant corner, far away from everyone else, where I could be alone with my own private sorrows. In some curious way that I could not explain, the dark cedar trees and sombre walls of the convent next door seemed to fit much more with the way I felt inside.

Several weeks later, when I had begun to despair of ever seeing my father again, one of the sisters stopped me as I was coming back through the convent gate after school. She sat me down by the sundial and took one of my hands in hers.

'I've got something bad to tell you,' she said. 'And we had best get it over with. It's about your father.' I remember not wanting to hear the next words and wishing that the whole world would stand still. But she continued, 'The hospital have told us that he may not live through the night, and he is calling for you to go and say goodbye.'

Most of that terrible day I have managed to blot out of my memory. But I know that we searched for something to take him and decided on a single, lovely clematis flower from the convent wall. Sister also produced a little lead cross from her pocket which she said would help him to think about our blessed Lord as he crossed over into everlasting life. I remember thinking that wherever 'everlasting life' was I wanted to go there too—and as soon as possible; for, certainly, there was nothing left to live for down here.

The rest of that day was too horrible to think about. We eventually found my father propped up on his hospital pillows. The bed was so high that I had to be lifted up to see him. His face was white and drawn—almost waxen in appearance. I remember that he smiled a brief smile at the clematis I had chosen for him—I like to think that it was a small oasis of beauty in his dark haze of pain. But already he seemed far away on another journey, and I could not wait to get away from a situation which terrified me. There was nowhere to go now, and it felt as though my whole world had come to an end.

When the nuns came to tell me, some time later, that my father had died, I could not even cry. They seemed to find my reaction very unnatural, but I was way beyond tears. All I can remember is a feeling of frozen numbness that dulled my senses but didn't remove the pain. Everything that went on around me seemed far away, as I withdrew within my own private prison of grief.

My father had apparently clung on to the threads of life until an adoption had been arranged for me. He never met my new 'parents' but left all the arrangements to my godmother, already in her seventies.

In time I came to love my new parents as my own, but life with them was seldom smooth; and, looking back, I can see that they depended on me far too much. Their own relationship was dangerously close to the rocks, and they separated for long periods throughout my childhood.

They had always longed for a child of their own, but the problem for me was they they simply could not bear me to have any 'past'. I was by then seven years old and had many memories and experiences burning inside me but it seemed vitally important to them that I should arrive, as it were, 'fresh off the shelf'. My father was deeply hurt if I so much as mentioned to anyone that I was adopted, and any attempt I made to talk about my life before I came to them was met with polite disinterested silence. I am sure that they did not intend to harm me in any way—it was just that they wanted a child who would be in every way, wholly and completely, 'their very own'. I imagine, too, that they had not the slightest idea of the resultant pain and grief that was to remain buried deep inside me for many, many years to come.

The extent of this total block on the natural working

out of my grief, and the lack of anyone to talk to about all that I had been through, was vividly illustrated when friends of ours adopted two little Vietnamese children a few years ago. They were brother and sister, just seven and five years old—and, of course, in the beginning they knew nothing but their own native tongue. Many times the little girl would awaken screaming with some terrible nightmare while her brother would hold her in his arms and comfort her. Often they would talk together for hours on end, sometimes crying, sometimes clinging to one another. As they learnt their new language my friends would overhear words like 'fire', 'ambulance' and 'bombs' interspersing their regular conversations. But as the months went by the nightmares gradually ceased, and their terrible experiences in the Vietnamese war, when both their parents had been killed by bombing raids, were seldom mentioned. Being able openly to talk and cry about their experiences together, as well as with their new parents, had gradually drawn the terrible grief and pain that they had lived through. Today they are happily and enthusiastically living life to the full—a couple of real little tearaways!

Of course, my own bereavement experiences did not begin to compare with all that those little ones have gone through; but, unlike theirs, my memories did not see the light of day and begin to be worked out of my system for more than twenty years; and, as I described in *Free to Be Myself*, it was only afterwards that I realised the extent to which they had overshadowed my whole life, like a dark, heavy canopy, completely blocking out any possibility of real joy or freedom, not to mention the light of God's love.

Probably my single most traumatic bereavement happened when I was just nineteen; on top of all that had gone before, it left me totally devastated.

His name was Patrick, and we had gone out together

for nearly the whole of my first year at university. At last I had found someone to love and to begin to enjoy life with, miles away from the problems and stresses of my war-torn home—and it was magic. I will not dwell on the times we spent together, but every moment of that long happy summer remains clearly etched in my mind together with the places—the old Roman harbour, the ruined cathedral, and the beautiful cliffs high above the sea on the Scottish coastline. At least no one can take memories away.

He was a second-year student, and I had not realised how vital his exams were to him. True none of us did a great deal of work, but we always had the September resits to fall back on. The trouble was that if you failed a single subject in the second year, you were out. But it was not until we met up outside the examination hall in September, that I realised with a sinking heart just how serious things could be for him.

When he wrote to say that he had failed one subject and was being sent down, I was devastated. For the whole of that next term he stayed up there, just to be with me—struggling to make ends meet, doing farming and odd jobs in order to pay the rent. But in the end, his father insisted that he return home to Northern Ireland to look for a proper job, and that was the last time I ever saw him.

His letters became more and more despairing as he began to realise for the first time the opportunities he had thrown away. I was too far away to help him and, try as I would, my letters did not seem to be enough to lift his spirits.

I heard nothing for a couple of weeks. Then, one morning, I found a letter in unfamiliar handwriting waiting for me on the hall table. That moment remains with me as if it had occurred only yesterday.

He had taken his own life with an overdose that must

have killed him instantly, his mother wrote. She enclosed a letter that he had left for me. In it he had written: 'I love you but I cannot go on. Somehow I know that you will succeed and survive without me but, as for me, I have thrown everything away and there is nothing left to live for.'

My sense of guilt and failure was almost overwhelming. Did he really not know just how much I needed him? Wasn't there something I could have done, even at this distance? Or was it me—with all the deaths that seemed to have followed me wherever I went? Was I somehow contaminated—a curse on all who came close to me?

This time I really did collapse with grief, retiring to the shelter of my darkened room, completely unable to face up to life any more. The doctor was very kind, coming often to see that I was sufficiently sedated, and my roommate did her best—but it was hopeless. I could not face the thought of life without him, and over and over again I cursed myself for not having helped him enough when he needed me. Exams were fast approaching, but I could not even think about them. The only reading I could face was sad poetry and anything that tried to express the grief I felt.

I was not a believing Christian at the time, although for many years I had attended the Catholic church as a matter of duty. One thing that concerned me was what would happen to Patrick now? I knew enough of the church's teaching to be aware that suicide was regarded as a mortal sin condemning one for eternity—but I could not bring myself to accept this. Surely there must be some mistake?

Eventually, having managed to drag myself out of bed and dress, I made my way round to see the Catholic priest. But any hopes of comfort from this source were soon dashed. Suicide was the ultimate never-to-be-forgiven sin; at that time, these unfortunate people were not even allowed a Christian burial. As I left the church that day I vowed never to go back—for if this was really what God was like then I certainly did not want to know him.

It was to be many years before I returned to God, through the loving compassion of a Christian friend. Mercifully today many churches have a more enlightened attitude towards the whole subject of suicide, recognising that the unbearable pressure that drives a man to this extremity is better regarded as a sickness than a sin. God alone knows what happens inside a person's heart at such desperate moments, and he is the ever-merciful judge.

When I returned home that summer, having well and truly failed my exams, I got little sympathy.

'Don't expect to become the tragedy queen here,' my mother said. 'Just get on with some work, and look to your own future.' I am sure that, like most of her generation, she really thought this was the best way to help, but yet again my grief had to go underground.

Many years later, during a Christian counselling course we were asked to share with the group anything that we could remember of our early childhood. When it came to my turn, I apparently told my story clinically and with complete detachment, as if it had all happened to someone else a very long time ago. After I had finished the group leader turned to me in amazement and asked, 'Don't you feel anything Ann? I can tell you now I shan't be happy until you become angry about all that has happened to you.'

I am sure that at the time I regarded her remark with deep suspicion, thinking it showed an extremely un-Christian attitude. Of course, she was absolutely right, as I was soon to find out! Anger and grief are much more closely linked than some of us realise, and sadly many bereaved people get caught in this nasty little trap. Their friends will often look on with horror as they express hurt and anger against the doctors, the relations who weren't there, and of course most frequently against God himself for removing the loved one from their midst. But if this so-called un-Christian feeling is suppressed, people are often prevented from fully working out the grief that is boiling away down below the anger.

Since the Son of God himself was prepared to bear the anger and bitterness of the whole world on his shoulders as he hung on the cross, then surely—as Scripture teaches—he is more than willing to bear this burden for us as well? Moreoever, since he knows everything that there is to know about us, then he knows and understands about the anger anyway.

Up until that moment I had accepted everything that had happened to me with hopeless resignation: the death of my own parents and that of my baby brother; my adoptive parents' stormy and frequently disintegrating marriage; my unhappiness throughout my schooldays as I struggled with this and with trying to meet their needs instead of my own; and then Patrick's suicide; it all just seemed to be my lot in life, and there was an end to it. This did not make me a very cheerful person to have around, but then I suppose this was hardly surprising!

With the extraordinary sense of timing that God so often displays, my latent anger was seething very close to the surface indeed at this particular time—though for a very different reason. My husband's job was taking him abroad for longer and longer periods, and I was often left alone to cope with our three growing children for six to eight weeks at a time.

In some way that I could not have explained, being constantly left on my own to cope with everything like this had come to represent all the bad things that had ever happened to me—the bereavements, the rejections and the loss of security.

I suspect that after that evening in the counselling group many of the people had been praying for me, because very shortly afterwards the time bomb that had been ticking away for so long in my innermost being finally exploded with almost volcanic force! Whereas previously I had meekly accepted everything without a murmur as my personal cross to bear, now suddenly I could no longer contain my anger at the seeming injustice of it all—the way I was left so often to cope with everything on my own, the children's needs that were not being met, any more than my own had been.

The anger itself was almost irrelevant, but acted as a sort of tension release for all the feelings that had remained bottled up inside me. It was like the tip of some gigantic iceberg beneath which lay all the endless grief that had been imprisoned for years; oceans of it, soaking every available handkerchief and making life in our house an extremely damp and rather embarrassing experience for many months.

As I cried and cried over every sad book and film, and often over nothing in particular, my poor husband could not begin to understand what was going on. It seemed that someone was leaning very hard on all these early wounds. My neighbour's husband was killed in a plane crash; a close friend from India, who had been like a mother to me, died quite unexpectedly in her early fifties, leaving me almost beside myself with grief at her funeral; then, one after another, the children's precious animals went as well: our beloved stripey cat just disappeared; my eldest daughter's tame duck was killed by a fox, and three little guinea pigs died within a matter of months. And of course, as I struggled to help the children cope with grief and death, I became more and more aware that I had never worked any of this out in my own life.

Suddenly I needed to be alone with my grief, and to go back through the years to find the places that I had known—the house where I had lived with my own parents, the graveyard where they were buried, the hospital where my mother had died. What were my parents like? Did they really love me? How could they have left me? The past suddenly reared up on my horizon with the most gigantic storm clouds, almost obliterating everything else from view. It was like a chapter in my life that had started but remained uncompleted all those years, and, come what may, I simply had to return to those pages in order to find healing.

The other day I came across something that I wrote in my diary at this time:

> *All round this churchyard lies the pain I feel,*
> *Pain that in the very stones cries out,*
> *For who can feel that loss which no man*
> *   living can replace?*
>
> *Beauty of grass and stone and moss unite,*
> *And mould a harmony so lovely that it hurts to*
> *   see,*
> *But who can feel that loss which only those*
> *   who live know well?*
>
> *The bell tolls on—its lingering note strikes pain*
> *   within my heart,*
> *Beneath this stone or that one, moss encrusted*
> *   they may lie,*
> *But can I ever feel the loss that is so far away?*

'It feels,' the diary continues, 'as if I want to stay here for ever within this fleeting glimpse of time—the beauty and the sorrow that lie here in the sunlight, beneath the echo of that bell. A little vase of primroses fresh beside the grave of someone still remembered says it all—but the hand of a small child still very much alive pulls me back into the cold clear light of today.

'I love her—I love them all, but all that is within me longs to stay awhile and grieve. What joy is there in life when there is so much pain? Why was I left behind when everyone that mattered to me went on ahead? Perhaps if I were to stay here I could find that peace, that oblivion which seems to offer all.'

But gradually as these monsoon months of rain and darkness passed, I began to discover a very strange thing. The first time I consciously noticed it, we were driving down one of those narrow lanes in the Surrey countryside where the branches of the beech trees form a living archway overhead, and the gnarled roots intertwine along the roadside. As I looked up at the spring green leaves, translucent with the sun shining through them, I could hardly believe my eyes—they were amazingly beautiful!

It was not that I had never seen them before; on the contrary, we had travelled this route many times. But now, for the very first time, they entered my innermost being in full glorious technicolour. It was as if the sheer weight of grief that I had carried for so long had been lifted from my shoulders, and I could actually see and feel for the first time in many, many years. Now suddenly I began to enjoy all kinds of things—friends, relationships, the beauty all around us, new experiences; it was as if I had begun to live at last!

As I have seen many times through my counselling work, shutting out pain inevitably shuts out life as well. We build a kind of armour-plating round ourselves to protect our vulnerability but we destroy so much more in the process. This is not to say that the wounds of bereavement ever disappear altogether, because they do not. Time distances, but it does not completely heal—

and the scars inevitably remain for others to trample on unwittingly if we allow ourselves to be vulnerable. After Patrick's death it took me many years to allow myself to risk loving again, and I have often deliberately kept people on the outside of my life—trusting only a very few. But if we want to live again, we must eventually take the risk of facing up to the pain, allowing ourselves to be vulnerable to those around us.

What difference has all this made to the way I live? Certainly experience has well and truly taught me to make the most of today. I never take anything or anyone for granted. We none of us know what accident or illness may suddenly overtake our loved ones or for that matter, ourselves. Never letting the sun go down on our wrath, making sure that our families know how much we love and value them, forgiving and forgetting resentments that were not really so important anyway—all these are not just good Christian principles, but vital ingredients in life, since none of us know what tomorrow may bring.

It has taken me a very long time to relax and begin to trust my heavenly Father with the safety of my loved ones—but he has given me very little choice. Gradually, almost imperceptibly, he has been showing me that, however hard it is to understand, he is the Good Shepherd, and he can be trusted with the well being of his sheep. As I write these words my husband is on his way to one of the nearby islands in a small plane, as a routine and regular part of his job. Next week our girls will be flying 12,000 miles to join us for Christmas. Every time, I commit them all yet again into his safe keeping, but it is never easy.

When the inevitable crises of life occur, I have constantly to struggle to remind myself that God is a loving Father, and that he does care what happens to me. The life experience of being orphaned can all too easily superimpose itself on my spiritual world, causing me to lose trust in the reality of a loving heavenly Father. At such times I have to go racing back to some of my favourite Bible verses, and to seek the comfort of the Rock that I know by faith and not by sight.

The greatest struggle I have had is with the question, 'Why?' and, 'How could a loving God allow all this to happen to one person?' And I imagine that I shall never find the answers this side of eternity.

The most helpful answer I ever received to this question came from a Christian counsellor, who just happened to be around when I was going through the thick of all this. He said, 'God needs men and women around who are deep and no one gets deep by accident. It's like the gold in the furnace—the more fire he can pass you through, the richer you become.'

That is not a very comforting answer, but I can certainly see it working out in other people. Without exception, those in whom the light and love of God shines the brightest have really been through the mill. They are 'real', genuine, caring, and there is nothing superficial about them. Instinctively I find myself drawn towards such people, and I suspect that the rest of the world does too.

Of course, we would all prefer the easy comfortable pain-free high roads—but then Jesus himself was 'a man of sorrows acquainted with grief', and maybe this is all a part of the painful life-long process of becoming more like him.

Wendy Green has written and published many books, but none has had greater impact than *The Long Road Home* (Lion Publishing), in which she recalled the terrible pain of watching her husband Peter die of cancer. Anne Watson says that she found this 'the most helpful book she had read since her husband David died'.

In this chapter she recalls many of the memories, and talks of how Peter's death affects her deeply even today.

Wendy has four children, ranging from the age of twenty-one to only seven, and she lives in Forest Gate just outside London.

It took her nearly three years before she could bring herself to write again following *The Long Road Home*— the experience was so desperately painful—but now she has started work on another project requiring a great deal of research.

Wendy tries to balance her life between supply teaching in the local school and finding enough time for the new book. She also finds a real sense of fulfilment in helping out with seminars on bereavement which have been run in her locality.

As I write this, it's three and a half years since my husband died, but I still had to come out of church one Sunday recently, because I couldn't hold back the tears. Much to my annoyance. And why? There had been no hassle with the children, no more anxieties than usual, nothing spectacular about the sermon. It wasn't the wrong time of the month. I wasn't overworked or over-tired or under stress. In fact we had only recently come back from holiday, and I was congratulating myself on feeling comparatively relaxed. Till we got to the last verse of the last hymn, and the second line read, 'We'll fight life's final war with pain.' Suddenly I was back in the thick of it, sitting in the lounge with Pete, during the last weeks of his life, re-living his battle with cancer of the stomach.

I could feel myself trembling, as I struggled to fight back the tears. I took deep breaths in a desperate effort to calm myself, and searched frantically through my pockets for a handkerchief. It was no use. I would have to make an undignified exit, or end in an even more undignified heap on the floor. My logical self knew that such feelings are normal, inevitable, a natural part of the grief process. There was no shame in sobbing my heart out in the ladies loo. A friend assured me it was 'early days'.

'Who is she kidding?' stormed my other self. The one that wants to be in control of any and every crisis, to never let the mask slip, never reveal the panic simmering barely beneath the surface. Early days—my foot! It's three and a half years. It's time I'd dealt with it, learnt to accept the unacceptable, made a new life for myself, let go of the past.

The trouble is the past has a horrible way of catching up with you, and slapping you in the face when you're least expecting it. A letter addressed to the person who has died. A photo. A television programme. A fragment of music. The line of a hymn. Crash. The barriers are down. Memory stares you hard in the eyes. You cannot erase someone you have loved, just like that, especially when there are children involved. If you don't remember, they surely will remind you, in personality and mannerisms, as well as words.

'It's sad our daddy died, isn't it?' reflects Jenny our seven year old at periodic intervals. There's no real answer to that, other than a hug, and a murmur of agreement. Mercifully it is a more generalised sense of sadness now, rather than the total devastation of that first year.

When a person of major importance in your life dies, it is as if your known world has stopped, though life somehow still seems to be going on all around you. Telephones ring, meals are prepared, people go about their daily business. You sit in the middle staring at a letter, or trying to focus your mind on forms and certificates, talk of widows and probate, flowers and funeral arrangements. Things which have nothing to do with you, or your family. Your lips might answer. Your hands move. The real me was looking over my right shoulder, watching, wondering: How does she do it? How can she carry on as though nothing has happened? What will happen when it really sinks in and the numbness wears off?

At least I had some preparation, some understanding

of what was going on in me. The year before, my father had died. Two years before that, my cousin had lost her husband and her little girl in a car accident. My family were no strangers to grief. I had sat with my cousin at 5.30 a.m. as, shocked and numb, she moved the pieces of a jigsaw into position, functioning on some form of remote control that knew where to place the pieces of the cardboard puzzle, but was giving few clues on how to reorganise the shattered fragments of her life. When I had been researching a book about divorce, divorcés had spoken of similar feelings; they had described what they were going through as akin to a bereavement experience. One after another had described the overwhelming emotions which they had found so much harder to handle than all the practical considerations. Even so, I had no real appreciation of how much it would hurt, how many old wounds would be re-opened, how vulnerable you become.

Over that first year, I felt rather like an onion, as layer after layer was peeled from my protective surfaces, exposing the real self inside, taking me right down to basics. Initially I think we all experienced a sense of relief mixed with the sadness. Peter had not been himself for over a year and the strain had been enormous, though we had not been informed that he had cancer, and that it was inoperable up to a matter of weeks before his death. In many ways, then, the situation eased. At least we knew what was the matter. We were in it together, fighting the symptoms rather than each other—most of the time. The grief was not so much for ourselves as for him waging his final war with the pain of letting go of all the things that had meant so much to him: committees, church, football, holiday activities, the car, a bath, his school, the family, his overwhelming energy, life itself. Yes. We were relieved: he was safe; out of it; no more indignities, sorrow or pain.

Tears there were in plenty, though those of us closest to him had shed ours over the preceding weeks and months. Now we were in limbo. We knew something had happened, something of enormous magnitude that was about to alter our entire world. We couldn't think what. Or rather, we didn't want to think. The implications were too overwhelming. Sufficient for each day were the minor devastations. There were only five places to set for the evening meal, instead of six. For some inexplicable reason, the garage door didn't grind open at the usual hour. There was no one to hug our adopted daughter with a special 'grr'. The man on the Honda with the red helmet wasn't Pete. He wasn't in church in his lay reader's robes. He wasn't in school. His secretary told us that. She had a new typewriter and couldn't bear to use it because she kept thinking how much he would have enjoyed playing around with it. He wasn't in Nefyn, the little Welsh village where we spent our summer holidays. He wasn't at home when we came back at the end of August.

Only then did reality begin to sink in. Four months after the main drama. Pete had gone. And he had gone for good. We couldn't tell him that David had passed his O levels, with very good grades, even though he had taken them only three weeks after his father's death. We couldn't hand over the application forms for a grant for sixth form college. It was I who was stuck in the study for three days, with David hardly daring to show his face round the door in case I burst into tears again, as I wrestled with income, outgoings, name of husband, status of husband. Should I put 'DECEASED' to get the message home! The reason for my anger, that sudden surge of energy when I must weed the garden, to take the dog for a walk, or clean the house. True measure of my desperation.

Why did you do it Pete? Why go and die? Why didn't

the doctors do something sooner?

What possible reason could you have for all this, God? And don't tell me suffering ennobles people. I might punch you on the nose. Or not you but those representatives of yours who think they have it all tied up in neat theological bundles, and aren't in there with the sufferer, sharing the darkness and the hurt. As you are. Taking the pain and the anger, showing me daily just how deep your love goes; that I need not try to hide from you: I do not have to pretend. You have an answer for the questions and accusations. You can help me deal with the memory of all the things I said, or didn't say, did or didn't do. All the 'if only's; with the guilt about how much I added to, rather than alleviated, Pete's problems; with the frustration and pain which otherwise might have driven me to alcohol, tranquillizers, a new relationship, a flurry of hyperactivity—anything to deaden hurt or still the mind.

Thank you that your hands are steady on the reins even if I go cavorting around like an unbridled filly, especially as the dreaded dates loom large on the horizon: birthdays, anniversaries, Christmas, the anniversary of his death. Pete died in May. The day he died the tulips and irises in our front garden were of such clarity; and the other world was so close that I almost felt that if I stretched out my hand too far, it would disappear into it. I still can't cope with the tulips and irises when they bloom each year. I don't know whether to dig them up, trample them down, or throw them over the wall into next door's garden. Jenny (our youngest daughter) has a similar problem. This year she was doing a project on spring flowers at school. She stood on the doorstep chanting a litany of flowers in our garden.

'What are those?' she asked pointing to a cluster of blue and pink.

'Forget-me-nots,' I replied, wincing, anticipating her

reaction. We had planted a clump of forget-me-nots for each of the children the week Pete died. Perhaps she wouldn't remember? She was only three at the time. I should be so lucky.

'Don't say that,' she said, burying her face in my skirt. 'They remind me of Daddy.'

Yes, Jenny. You do the same to me. The broad shoulders, pouting lips, agile brain, boundless energy, determined will. He is going to be with us for a very long time. Only you can't say that to a six year old. You just gulp, and arrow a quick prayer for the right words, or action, then find some means of steadying yourself before the next blow falls. You sometimes begin to feel a bit like one of these kelly dolls we had after the war. Round-bottomed plastic things you could knock over, but they always righted themselves. I just about stabilise when the next shock comes. Maybe not quite so often now, but daily, hourly, in those first few months. Is it any wonder that people don't want to get up, don't want to go to bed, don't want to face the reality of adjusting their mental and emotional map over and over again? Depression sets in if there is no outlet to express the sadness welling up inside; if you think you must suppress your feelings because of the children, or other people's unrealistic expectations.

One of my greatest concerns was that, on the day of her Dad's funeral, one of my daughters, who hadn't been able to cry previously, was told, 'You've got to be brave. For your mother's sake.' We are still reaping the fruits. I bottle my feelings to some extent still, but I have learned a new freedom, that of telling God exactly what I think and feel. I can pour out my grief and resentment, like Hannah, and the psalmists, in full knowledge that he won't reject or abandon me. His shoulders are broad enough to take it. He knows and understands the pain of someone good gone from his world. He has taught me that grief is the price we pay for loving.

There is no way round grief. The tablets and alcohol can only numb the ache for so long. The fevered activity must come to a halt sooner or later. Depression may push you to thoughts of suicide or lead to mental illness if the root cause is not acknowledged. Bereavement hurts. Loss of a partner through death or divorce come high on the stress ratings. The bereaved are not going to 'snap out of it', or 'get over it' once the funeral is out of the way, and everything is back to 'normal'.

The whole of that first year was like riding an emotional switchback, as I hauled myself (or rather God hauled me by the scruff of the neck) to the top of the slope, only to disappear down the other side at a rate of knots. I could joke about scattering a few rainbows round the kitchen. In reality it was no joke as I plunged from tears to laughter, from the heights to the depths. Often wondering quite what effect it was having on the children but seemingly powerless to do anything. It all took so much energy. How could I think myself into their minds when half the time I didn't know what was going on in my own? Even baking a cake, or whipping up a pudding was beyond me.

Jenny's comments were painful but in many ways, I guess, she has helped us to identify and come to terms with our grief. Somehow a four-year-old doesn't have quite the same inhibitions as a fourteen-year-old or as a widow (I still hate that word) in her forties. She, and my mum, and my cousin, taught us the value of talking, of putting feelings into words, of not switching off and pretending the person who died never existed.

'You lot talk so freely about Pete, I keep expecting him to come into the room,' commented a friend a few weeks after Pete's death. He still creeps into the conversation with unfailing regularity, but not with the compulsion of those early days. It's as if you have to talk to get it

out of your system, make some sense of the whirl of
emotions and difficulties that are spinning round in your
brain. Friends worry that they won't know what to say.
Often their fears are groundless. All you need is someone to listen, and help point you in the right direction.

Income tax and grant forms are still my major stumbling block, along with patching up the car, keys that
break off in locks, and all the minor maintenance jobs
that no one wants to know about. I make no apologies to
my feminist friends. I know an awful lot of men who
have similar problems, and doubt that Pete would have
fared any better if he had been left to cope as mother/
father/homemaker/provider/gardener/unattached youth
worker/chief cook and bottle-washer. He too would have
needed some support system, an occasional hug of encouragement, a shoulder to cry on when the kids and the
work and the coping alone get on top of you. It's not that
you rely on somebody being alongside you twenty-four
hours a day, but it does help if there are folk around who
don't just ask, 'Is there anything I can do?' but assess the
need and do it. If there is someone at the end of the
street or the end of the telephone you can offload some
of the emotions on to, all the better.

'I'm back on those wretched tablets again,' I stormed
down the phone to my main prop a few months after
Peter's death.

'Quite frankly, I'm surprised you haven't been on
them before,' came her calm reply. Those who can take
the anger and frustration, who make some attempt to
appreciate how they would feel if their partner had died
and their world had disintegrated, do more than they will
ever know for those finding themselves very difficult
people to live with.

'I went to visit a neighbour who had lost her husband,'
said one of my friends. 'I got really wound up about it. I
didn't know what to say, so I only popped in for a few

minutes.' Three hours later she emerged. The woman had been so desperate for someone to talk with, someone to whom she could pour out the confusion of events and feelings.

Not that everyone will want to unburden themselves all the time or to anybody. I think you choose your people, the ones you feel safe with, who, you are confident, will not make facile judgements or comments. You avoid those who spout clichés, or texts, or tell you God is going to teach you all kinds of things, when God has been working overtime on you for the last twelve months. You learn to blank off to that kind of consolation, to build up your own set of defence mechanisms.

When my father died my mother couldn't get his car out of the drive fast enough. It was too painful a reminder: I am here, but my owner is not. We clung on to Peter's car. I felt safe in it, and only agreed to sell it when it was gobbling petrol at the rate of fourteen miles to the gallon. My father died suddenly with a heart attack. My mother didn't want to look at a photograph album for months after his death. The first thing I did was to put several of Pete's photos in prominent positions to restore the image of the person we had known before his illness took hold. Both my mother and I find church services undermine our defences faster than anything. There are so many hymns you associate with another time, another place; so many images centred on death and resurrection; music that reaches the parts a sermon can never touch. I have a new coping mechanism now. When I see a line, a verse, that is likely to come too close for comfort I leaf through my book for a hymn which is less distressing. My mouth might open and close in the appropriate places but my mind is as far removed as possible.

'Time heals,' soothe the comforters. 'It gets better.' It doesn't feel like it during that first year, or when you are

suddenly precipitated back into the past as I was that
Sunday morning.

'It doesn't get better,' commented a friend whose
father had died. 'You just learn to live with it.'

The experts assure you that the final stage of grief is
that of acceptance. Whatever that means. The closest I
can get is a reluctant acknowledgment that all this has
happened. I still hassle with God along the lines of
'Why?' and 'How could you?' I'm not joking when I tell
people that when my time comes I will go galloping
through the gates of heaven demanding. 'O.K., God.
Now will you explain?' Of course, I know that explanations will be unnecessary, that the glimpses we catch in
our less argumentative moments will no longer seem like
fragments seen through a glass darkly. It will all fall into
place. But I'm not there yet. The imagery of Psalm 23 is
very appropriate. The valley of the shadow of death is
dark and deep, for those who go through into bright
sunlight, and for those who are left behind.

I have an updated translation of an Eastern saying
pinned by my desk: 'If you want to get rid of the darkness you turn on the light.' In the early days after Peter's
death I couldn't bear harsh light. Or loud music. Even
the radio or television. It's as if part of you is still linger-
ing on the edge of that other world. You don't want the
distractions that will pin you back to earth or inquisitive
searchlights probing your innermost secrets. All you can
bear is the soft flickering of a candle; a gentle light beside
you in the darkness, and equally fragile. Then slowly,
imperceptibly, when you have almost given up hope, a
faint glimmer of dawn flushes the horizon, bringing with
it the gradual realisation that there may be a possibility
of new beginnings. The sun will shine again, however
many rainbows may temporarily blur your vision—even
after three and a half years.

6   **After a Lifetime**   *George Duncan*
           Together

The Rev. George Duncan was educated in Scotland and
served for three years as curate at Broadwater Church in
Worthing, Sussex. He was subsequently at St James's,
Carlisle, St Thomas's, Edinburgh, and Christ Church,
Cockfosters. He then returned to Scotland, serving for
six years at Portland Church in Troon, and for twelve
years at St George's Tron Church in Glasgow.

He is an internationally-known preacher and has
spoken regularly at the Keswick Convention since 1947,
at the Filey Christian Holiday Crusade since 1955, and at
similar conventions all over the world.

He is the author of several devotional books.

Some fifteen months have passed since my wife Catherine was suddenly called Home, but as I write this chapter I find that the wounds have scarcely begun to heal. Someone once said to me that the second year of bereavement can be even worse than the first, and I am beginning to believe that he was right.

In the first place, I want to look at 'facing bereavement', as I have had to do for nearly fifty years alongside others who have been bereaved. I wonder how many funeral services I have conducted, how many homes I have entered where a loved one has been taken. That long experience has taught me, I trust, quite a few lessons. The first is how individual, how intimately personal a matter, bereavement is. Circumstances differ so much. For some who have watched a loved-one face a long, weary road of suffering, of pain and, sometimes, of physical and mental deterioration, death has come with almost a sense of relief that rest and peace have come at last. Of course there is sadness and even deep sorrow, but that is mingled with thankfulness that the end has come. In other cases, when a little child has been taken, or a husband or wife after just a few years of married life and happiness, the hurt is almost unbearable and words are futile.

Other lessons have, I trust, been learned. The first is

the need for the most thorough pastoral care. This must be shown in the visiting of the home before and after the service and during the service itself. We have to learn to 'weep with those that weep'. This can be costly in terms of time and of sharing deeply in the sorrow. Sometimes our tears might mean more than our words. We also have to learn to withhold our judgment at times. I remember clearly being asked to visit a young married man who was dying. He knew it, though he was determined not to die, and the family knew it and were all in tears. I was told that he was a communist, and that meant that he was an atheist. Did that mean that he was a lost soul going to a lost eternity? We talked and then we prayed. I held his hand in mine as I prayed. I thanked God for all that Christ had done for us in his death and resurrection. Every time I mentioned the name Christ, his hand tightened on mine! I was told afterwards that when he had been a young man he had been 'very religious', a phrase I find is often used to describe someone who has been a true Christian. I am sure that when he knew that he was facing death, his faith in the Saviour was quickened again in the hour of his need.

What do we say or think when we face the situation where a Christian wife has prayed for an unbelieving husband, or a Christian son or daughter has prayed for an unbelieving mother or father? I'm not sure that we can say anything except that God certainly heard their prayers, just as he will have heard any cry—however last minute or faint—from their loved ones and that he will act with perfect justice and mercy.

Some if not most bereavements leave wounds which take a very long time to heal, and this should make us slow in our judgement of people of whose background we know little. I remember one family: the mother attended church with one of her daughters but the other daughter never came. I had judged her to be hard.

But one day I discovered that she was deeply hurt. I already knew she was a widow, but I had no idea that her marriage had lasted only a few days. She had married a pilot in the R.A.F. in World War Two. He returned to duty almost immediately after the wedding, and was reported 'missing, presumed dead'. She wasn't hard: she was hurt—badly hurt.

The death of a child or a baby is possibly the saddest thing that can happen. I dreaded taking such a service in case emotion would overwhelm me and I would break down. Two thing have steadied me in my thinking at times like these. One was a saying of my own father: 'Heaven wouldn't be home, if there were no children there.' The other was something that the Rev. R. A. Finlayson once said in a country parish at the funeral of a little child. He said that if, in going from one pasture to another, the sheep hesitated in fear at a narrow bridge over a stream in flood, the shepherd would go to the flock, pick up a lamb and carry it to the other side. Immediately the mother would follow, and this would encourage the others to do the same. The action of the shepherd in carrying a lamb across first would make it easier for the flock to cross over.

All this might well be true, but there remain the harsh facts of the child's empty bed, of his unworn clothes and unused toys, and of his voice no longer heard. How rightly the Bible speaks of death as the 'last enemy'. But the verse which names death as the enemy ends with the word 'victory'. When taking a service of this nature, I focus on the sure and certain hope which Christ brings.

Of life after death, someone has said that a universal instinct believes in it, a moral necessity demands it and *an historical fact proclaims it*.

In one of my two favourite talks given at funerals, I point out three 'not's in the Bible. When our Lord went into the home of Jairus where a little girl had died, he said, 'She is *not dead*.' The second 'not' comes in one of the accounts of the resurrection of Christ when the women went to the tomb to weep and to mourn and were met with the words, 'He is *not here*.' The third 'not' came from the lips of Christ when the disciples did not understand what he was doing or why and he said, 'What I do thou knowest *not now*, but thou shalt know hereafter.' 'Not dead . . . not here . . . not now!'

The other talk is based on the words of Christ, 'Let not your heart be troubled neither let it be afraid . . . I go to prepare a place for you.' I suggest that death always troubles our minds, if we think at all, and that Christ, and Christ alone, can speak peace to our troubled hearts. We can be troubled at the thought of our *sinfulness*: the knowledge that we are not fit to meet God; but Christ answers that through his death upon the cross for our sins. We can be troubled at the thought of the *loneliness* of death: when we die, we die alone; but the Christian is not alone. The words of the 23rd Psalm leap to our minds, 'Yea though I walk through the valley of the shadow of death, I will fear no evil for *thou art with me*, thy rod and thy staff they comfort me. Goodness and mercy shall follow me all the days of my life (and then I will die? No—that's not what the psalmist says. He continues, instead:) and I will dwell in the house of the Lord for ever.' Then we are troubled by our helplessness; but Christ tells us that his love has prepared a place and that we shall be with him.

The bereavement of others that I have had to face as a clergyman, has not been an easy part of my work, but it is at such times that I am made to realise my total dependence on Christ. Apart from him, we have no assurance and no hope.

But bereavement comes closer, sooner or later, to us all in our family circles and then it takes on an added dimension. Being a member of a fairly large family, with uncles, aunts, cousins, brothers and sisters, death came into my life on several occasions. The first that I can recall, was the death of my elder sister at the age of twenty-eight. She had been ill with T.B. of the spine for four years, nursed by my mother who was a trained nurse. What dedication that entailed! To the best of my knowledge, she never took a day or a night off duty. I was on holiday with a friend in North Wales when a telegram arrived: 'Come home at once Puss very ill.' I caught the first train I could. Before changing trains at Craven Arms Junction, I phoned home to be told that she had gone. I got home in the early hours of the morning and, for the first time in my life, saw death and felt the coldness of my sister's body as I kissed her. But as I went into the room, God gave me the words of the first Easter: 'He is not here . . . She is not here.' This seemed to take a weight off my mind and heart. Upstairs, I met my mother coming out of her bedroom, and I looked at her hands and thought that now they would be empty after four years' caring for her firstborn. On the day of the funeral, a short service was held in our drawing-room before the service in my father's church. My father and I went in to see Puss before the coffin was closed. I remember his words as we left the room where her body lay, 'With another body next time, thank God.'

I have vague memories of the church service and the singing of the hymn, 'How bright those glorious spirits shine,' and of feeling deeply moved by the words. Then came the long walk of two miles to the cemetery where she was to be buried. My father told me she had made one request to him just before she had died: that she should not be buried until four days after her death. Was it the fear that she might be buried alive? A member of the congregation said that when she heard the news, her first thoughts were, 'Poor Puss!' Then she realised how wrong it was to talk like that of one who had reached the glory of heaven.

When my mother died, I had little warning. One Sunday, I answered the telephone in our rectory in Edinburgh, to be told that she had been taken ill and rushed into the Royal Infirmary. I went there immediately. Her bed was surrounded by screens and she was not conscious. After a little while, a nurse came and told me that I would have to leave as the doctor wanted to find out what the matter was. It had been a dull day but, as I was leaving her bedside, the sun broke through the clouds and a beam of sunshine spread across her bed. As I walked away, the words that came into my mind were, 'At evening time, it shall be light.' For her it was to be the everlasting light and day of glory. Shortly after I got home, the phone rang. She had died. The evening service was to be the first in a special series and at such short notice I could not opt out of it. It was one of the most difficult services at which I have preached, but God gave me the needed grace.

My father's death was also sudden, although he had reached his eightieth year, looked after by my sister, one of that noble band of daughters who care for old folk with amazing devotion. He had a stroke. I hurried out to his home, then followed the ambulance to the Deaconess Hospital. It travelled fast and the journey was almost too much for my father, as he was swung this way and that. My brother and sister were already at the hospital. As the evening drew on, the nurse suggested that there were not likely to be any developments in the night, so my brother and sister went home while I stayed.

Two memories linger in my mind. The first is of how weak and helpless my father was. I had to hold the cup which had a spout to make drinking easier. I realised then that there had been a time when I had been helpless too, in my infancy and childhood, and that for years my mother and father had had to take care of me. What a debt I owed to them, and what a minute part of that debt I was being asked to repay then! I suddenly noticed that his breathing was getting gentler, quicker and shallower; then it ceased. This was the first and the only time in my life that I have seen anyone die and death come as gently as sleep—for which I was thankful.

The other memory concerns talking with my sister some days later, when she mentioned, quite casually, how my father had lived for my letters! She did not mean the comment critically but the words stuck in my mind, making me wish that I had written more. I have few memories of the service in the church of which my father had been minister: Tynecastle Parish Church, with a membership then of over two thousand but, sadly, closed down now.

When Catherine, my wife, died on the 26th August 1985, her death had a totally different impact on me. It was absolutely shattering because it was so totally unexpected and because we had been together for almost forty-six years. On Sunday, the 18th, she had complained of chest pains in the morning, but when I suggested getting the doctor, she would have none of it, assuring me that she would be all right. I was in a dilemma, as I was due to speak that Sunday morning at a conference at Oakhill College and again in the evening. She wanted me to go and, reluctantly, I did—having decided to return after the morning session and record the evening message. This I did; I also went to see my son who lived only a mile away, and told him that his mother was not well. He and his wife Jennifer went round at once and took Catherine to the doctor. Her own doctor was not available and this doctor's diagnosis was 'angina', for which Catherine was given some little pills to put under her tongue when the pain returned. I was home by early afternoon, but I did not know until later, that when John and Jennifer had arrived, they had found Catherine in tears. That memory still hurts, as I find myself asking whether I should have stayed with her and not gone to the conference.

At the first opportunity, we went to see her own doctor. He confirmed that it was angina, gave her more tablets and arranged for her to have an E.C.G. examination at Queen Victoria Hospital in East Grinstead, on the Friday. The report came on Saturday that everything was clear and there were no problems. That same day we went to my younger son's home at Penn and I left Catherine there while I went on to speak at some meetings nearby. Catherine was her usual self and gave no signs of any discomfort. The next morning, Sunday, at about 8 o'clock, she felt the pains coming back and sat up at the side of the bed. I phoned her own doctor, who came at once and changed the pills. He advised two days' rest in bed. We spent that Sunday resting together, little knowing that it was to be our last day. We watched the services on television and Catherine seemed to be in no discomfort. We went to sleep and I was wakened at 6.30 a.m. by the sound of her falling. I found her lying on the floor at the far end of the passage having just come out of the bathroom. She was dead. In falling, she had cut her head and there was a trickle of blood on the carpet.

I phoned the doctor who confirmed that she must have had a massive coronary, and said that, mercifully, she would not have known anything about it. Her death would have caused her fall, and the small amount of blood that had come from the wound in her head indicated that the heart had already stopped beating.

Then came the heart-breaking task of phoning the family with the message, 'Mummy has gone.' What happened throughout that day is beyond recall. I remember the doctor phoning the undertaker, and their coming to take her body away, to be brought back just a week later, before the service in our lovely little church.

The week was full of things that had to be done—all a merciful provision, because they help to occupy the mind. There were the practical matters to attend to: visiting the undertaker to choose the coffin; of letting people know; reading and answering the hundreds of letters that kept pouring in. How deeply moving to read these letters—hurtful, too! Kindness is the hardest thing to bear in such circumstances and yet what would we do without it? Then there were the arrangements for the funeral, including asking special friends to share in the service with the vicar. We felt that flowers should be confined to the family but some others did send them; among these was a magnificent floral arrangement from Japanese friends in Tokyo. Everywhere there was a sense of deep shock that Catherine had died, having apparently been so well and then going so suddenly.

I feared that we would not have many at the service: we had moved from Scotland nearly nine years previously so most of our friends lived a long way off, and many would not hear the news until it was too late. But people came and filled the church and God gave us a beautiful service. The vicar took it with great sensitivity and the lessons were read by a former colleague of mine in my church in Glasgow. He had travelled down in a friend's car the previous day and his presence meant much to me. Another friend led the prayers beautifully. One lady, a Roman Catholic, said she wondered if the church had ever heard singing like that before adding, 'What a difference it makes when those singing are all Christians!' The hymns were, 'The King of love my shepherd is', and 'Love divine all loves excelling'. The journey to the grave was a short one, barely a hundred yards from the door of the church to the little churchyard. The bearers walked rather more quickly than we did, but little Emily stuck close behind them. Just six years old, she wanted to keep as close to Granny as she could. Those who had come a distance were invited to our house nearby. The garden had all been prepared for them but a slight drizzle started and that meant that everyone had to come inside. It gave us and them the opportunity to talk and to say thank you. I was especially touched at the way the churchyard and the grounds round the church had been prepared. The church was without a verger at the time but several men turned up of their own accord to cut the grass and make everything beautiful. How much such kindness and thoughtfulness mean!

We had brought Catherine's body back home earlier in the day. It lay resting quietly in our lounge. The flowers from the family made the room look beautiful and the sun was shining in. The three granddaughters peeped in from the door; it all looked so lovely. They could not see Granny—just a curl of her white hair showed above the edge of the open coffin. I said to them that the body we have on earth is no use for heaven, so God has to give us another body.

There were, of course, many who had not been able to come and so another letter had to be sent out. In it I suggested that it would be a lovely thing if, as a result of Catherine's dying, others might live, and that a Catherine Duncan Memorial Fund should be set up under the control of T.E.A.R. Fund, The Evangelical Alliance Relief Fund—a charity which cares for the physical as well as the spiritual needs of young and old in many lands. As India had been the land of my birth and as my first four years of life had been spent in Calcutta, T.E.A.R. Fund were more than willing to foster the project. They knew of a choice bit of work being done by Rose and Wai Hu, that of caring for children in Calcutta. Little did we realise what the outcome would be. The gifts started coming in, and have continued to do so, until the total, at the time of writing, is close on £15,000.

This is being invested in the United Kingdom and the interest will be used to care for the children in Calcutta who otherwise would almost certainly have died. It takes only £100 to keep a child for a whole year, and £300 a year to train a Christian girl to be a nurse. As Catherine had been a nurse, we felt this would be a wonderful thing to take part in. So something positive has emerged out of something seemingly so completely negative. This has also given me something creative to do in the months following Catherine's death. I have tried to acknowledge in my own handwriting every gift that has been sent either to me or to T.E.A.R. Fund. Death has well been described in Scripture as our last enemy, but out of seeming defeat victory will come, and scores of children will be saved, not only physically but also spiritually, to serve Christ in that desperately needy land of India.

Death is, of course, the final challenge to our faith. Here the Christian has to fall back totally upon Christ, the merits of his death for our sins, and the historical fact of the empty tomb. The journey on is hard; the empty and silent house is not easy to live with. But it is wonderful to have a loving and caring family including children and grandchildren. It must be hard for anyone without that source of comfort, although the fellowship of the family of God will help to fill such a gap.

Fortunately, being a retired clergyman, I have never lacked opportunities for continuing to serve my Lord; and to be kept busy is one of the blessed factors that keeps the mind from dwelling too much upon the loss suffered. When we get into 'borrowed time', we know that it will not be long before, in the mercy and grace of God, we shall 'see those angel faces smile, which [we] have loved long since and lost awhile'. That hope is the final thing that enables me to continue until the same call comes for me; and if God in his mercy takes me in the same way that he took my beloved, I will be grateful.

The shock for those left behind is numbing, but later on, one is able to see how merciful it is to be spared weary months or years of pain and suffering before being 'absent from the body, but present with the Lord' and 'with Christ, which is far better'.

7   It Can't Be True!   *William White*

At the time of writing William White is nineteen years old and studying for a Diploma in Business Studies at Oxford Polytechnic. He also has to work three nights a week in a nightclub, which he does not find very edifying, but at least it pays for his studies!

He has been a Christian for seven years and has actually enjoyed this! In Oxford he goes to St Aldate's Church.

He has one sister, one half-sister, and another on the way, and he and they live near Burnham in Buckinghamshire.

His hobbies are singing, acting, writing and fly-fishing. He also enjoys helping other people and finds he is not bad at this.

Although it is five years since my mother died, I can still remember the exact scene at the moment when I heard the news. We were having a history lesson in one of the old classrooms on the east side of the school, and the smell of wood and dust basking in the April sunlight still lingers clearly in my memory. I was sitting next to my friend Charles Taylor and we were just messing around.

As the door at the back of the classroom opened and I saw the look in my housemaster's eyes, I knew exactly what had happened. They excused me from the lesson and I followed him up to the top of the school drive. We both stood on the grass looking out in the direction of the main road, with the silence wrung out between us. We stood there for what seemed an eternity, with the sound of the cars on the road droning past us. I felt totally alone. As the full realisation of what had happened began to penetrate, I could feel the tears welling up in my eyes. It was at this point that I asked God to help me: 'Please Lord take this terrible pain away—I know that the news will not change, but please help me to be strong and stay with me.' It was as if the Lord held me in his arms until that night when the hard cold truth finally dawned: my mother was dead and I would never see her again in this life.

My mother's death was part of a great bundle of hurt that I was to experience in the early part of my life. When I was only eleven, my father broke the news to me that Mum was having a nervous breakdown. I found it a very frightening thought, and it heralded the realisation that my parents were not as strong and impregnable as I had imagined them to be. I suppose that for all of us, when we are little, 'Father' seems the strongest man around, and 'Mother' is like some sort of superwoman. But 'superwomen' don't have nervous breakdowns!

The next cold fact of life presented to me, was that my parents were about to be divorced. The news broke on St David's Day, and my diary simply records the entry: 'Mum is about to divorce Dad—cried all night.'

The divorce was a very hard one indeed for everyone concerned, involving many sleepless nights for my sister and me. We were both totally disillusioned by our parents. The cotton-candy land, where everyone loves everyone else within the family circle, was shattered for ever. Instead there seemed only a bare landscape full of nasty unexpected pitfalls, where once there had been fountains of joy. As a child of this unsuccessful marriage, I suddenly found that I had become 'William, son of that awful woman' or of 'that terrible man', and, as relations took sides, our unspoken fears increased.

My mother married another divorcé with four children of his own, and she was also given custody of my sister and myself. But, since Mum died during the first year of their marriage and I was away at boarding school for much of the time, I never really got to know this new family, most of whom I resented, anyway.

My father married a much younger woman, who had no experience to equip her for looking after two newly-acquired teenagers. We disliked her because she could not do what Mum did; probably we never even gave her a chance. She and my father lived together before they got married.

It was on their wedding day that I took my first step on the path towards meeting the living God for myself. As they left for Paris on their honeymoon, my sister and I went with an uncle to a Christian family houseparty at a school near Basingstoke. By the end of that week, I had made a personal commitment to Christ, and his Holy Spirit had come to live within me.

Christmas came, bringing with it the one silver lining granted to the children of divorced parents—two lots of presents and two Christmas dinners! The pain always came afterwards, as we had to leave one parent to stay with the other.

The Lent term at Shiplake College found me in good form. I was reading my Bible regularly and I had signed on to be confirmed the following Christmas. In addition, I was among the top four oarsmen in the school, and the third fastest at cross-country running.

'Isn't life great!' I thought. 'Plenty of friends, success in a number of different fields . . .'

During the first half of term I was told that Mum was in hospital with back trouble. But it was only a minor kind of shock—after all modern medicine was so good that I knew for certain she would be fine soon.

One day at lunchtime, I was walking back to my house with a bookcase that I had made for my mother, when I recognised a car that was coming in at the top gate of the school.

'What on earth is my father doing here at this time?' I wondered, with a sinking feeling inside that something must be badly wrong.

Five minutes later, I was sitting in my housemaster's study staring straight past my father's head through a window, at a garden wall. The words being spoken at that time are still clear in my head, together with the terrible emptiness which engulfed me as I tried to take in the full implications of what I was being told.

Mum had got cancer all over her body. In fact, as I heard later, the doctor had said that, she was 'riddled with it, like woodworm in an old chair'.

'Everyone is doing all they can,' my Father said, 'but I think you must face the fact that she will most likely die.'

My father obviously expected some kind of emotional reaction, but as I sat gazing fixedly at the wall with a hopeless sick feeling inside without saying a word, he eventually continued, 'Don't worry too much. Everyone is doing all they can, but just prepare yourself for the worst.'

The rest of that lunchtime remains a blur, and even now I still can't remember what happened afterwards. School routine continued as before, mercifully acting as some kind of anaesthetic to numb my senses. But I did pray—crying out to God to heal Mum. Then, towards the end of term, my father turned up again to take me to see Mum in hospital. She might not last through the night, he told me, and she wanted the family with her. God had finally let me down I thought; despite all my desperate prayers to him, my mother was still going to die.

When I saw her lying there, in her hospital bed, it was the most terrible shock. I could hardly recognise the face that I had seen as recently as that half-term. The shape of her skull was clearly visible with the skin pulled tightly over her cheeks and forehead. Her eyes seemed twice their normal size and her lips were swollen and puffy, and covered in horrible dry scabs.

During those few first moments, the full horror of cancer struck home to me. That lovely face, once so bright and glowing with happiness, was now dull and cracked like a dried-up river bed desperate for water.

My mother woke up at the sound of our arrival, and tried to give us a reassuring wave—which was clearly a terrible effort for her. When she smiled, she seemed, somehow, like a young child trapped in an old and run-down body.

She needed help to struggle into a sitting position, and the nightie which I had seen so often before seemed suddenly like a giant's robe wrapped around her shrunken form. Her collar bones protruded painfully, and her arms were so thin that the elbow joints seemed huge in comparison. Like a tiny baby's, her neck seemed scarcely able to support the weight of her head. Her movements were slow and ponderous, like those of a very old pensioner, and every word seemed a terrible effort, as if she were fighting to control her own tongue.

We sat and talked, trying to make the most of our last few hours together, but it was almost impossible to hold back the tears—even though I knew how much my crying would affect her. She called me over and did her best to reassure me, but her very weakness spelt out the inescapable facts.

We left soon after that, and sat up at home, waiting for the phone to ring with the dreaded news. All that night I begged the Lord to save her; I'm sure I was not alone in this plea. The phone never rang, and my mother didn't die that night—and this was the best answer to prayer I ever had.

Amazingly, Mum seemed to get better and better, as the radiation and the chemotherapy began to take effect. All our relations and many prayer groups were lifting her up to God each day throughout this time. Mum was becoming quite a star in the hospital, and everyone who came into contact with her remarked that they had never seen anyone so happy as she seemed to be in the face of such terrible illness.

It was during this time that my mother had a visitation from God that came in the form of a dream, and her husband had exactly the same vision that very morning.

He saw a glowing crown of thorns, with my mother's face coming back from the darkness into the light through the centre of this. My mother had the same picture, but there were also two hands meeting and pulling each other from the darkness to the light.

There was never any question in my mind about the reality of this vision. It made me feel that God was working very closely with my mother and it seemed to me that she was getting better day by day enfolded in his loving care.

I spent most of that holiday with my father in Windsor, taking the occasional trip over to the hospital. My mother seemed visibly better each time. The only thing I found really difficult was how slurred and disjointed her words seemed to be, but I was told that this was only to be expected in view of the narcotic cocktail she was being given to ease the pain.

Throughout this time I was very aware of the closeness of God and the way he was aiding my mother's recovery. A wheelchair was delivered to the house to await my mother's return. Not only was this piece of equipment the most wonderful sign that she was definitely coming home, but it was also a great toy for me to play with! This was fine, until I skidded on the carpet leaving the most enormous and unmistakable rubber burn, which I duly had to pay for.

That Easter was one of the best holidays of my life. Mum was improving daily and full of excitement about returning home. She was already strong enough to walk across the room, and she could speak much more freely without the terrible dryness in her mouth. Her face and her body were filling out again, and the old sparkle had returned to her eyes.

As I returned to school that summer term, I began to relax, safe in the knowledge that my mother was well and happy again. She gradually slipped into the back of my mind, as my world became filled once more with summer games and all my friends. I didn't seem to need God so much either, and he quickly slipped into the background as well.

At about this time, a friend of my mother's went to see a medium to ask if Mum would live, and if her business would continue. The medium assured her that she would live, using the vision that my mother had had on which to base her prophecy.

Only a few days later, my mother died, despite the fact that she had been due to come home in two weeks' time.

I still find myself questioning why my mother died so suddenly and unexpectedly, and for a long time I was very angry with God. But two things kept coming to mind as I asked him, again and again, the reason for this happening.

We had all allowed God to drift into the background of our lives, the minute we thought my mother was finally better—and this is something I personally need to remember, because I frequently do forget about him when things are going well.

The second thought is that communication with evil forces is never right. If God had allowed my mother to live, would this have proved the medium right and reinforced the powers of darkness?

Probably, we shall never know for sure the real reason for my mother's death, this side of eternity, but I certainly wish that the two things I have just mentioned had never happened.

Sadly, after my mother's death, I lost contact with many people on her side of the family, but those who do keep in touch are a real blessing in the way that they care for my sister and me.

Even today I am still very much aware of God's presence with me, caring for me and disciplining me. When I occasionally drift away from the pathway, he still welcomes me back with open arms. And, despite the fact that he took my mother away at such an early age, I really love him and feel close to him—and you can only say things like that about very special friendships!

The Bible verses that helped me most through the time of my mother's death come from Mark chapter 4 verses 35 to 40. The last verse says it all for me, at times when I am faced with seemingly impossible hardships: 'Then Jesus said to his disciples, "Why are you so frightened? Have you still no faith?"' This always helps me to look back and remember the many things he has done for me in the past and so to trust that he will continue to help me in the years ahead.

Ann and Alastair Hubbard live in Sevenoaks where they are members of the local parish church of St Nicholas and very involved in the life there.

Ann originally trained and worked as a teacher, and she is now a governor of the local church primary school as well as a long-term member of the PCC.

Together, she and her husband have organised and run Bible study groups for many years, and Ann enjoys speaking to women's groups up and down the country.

Alastair is now self employed, having taken early retirement in order to act as consultant to a number of different Christian organisations.

In addition to looking after their elderly parents, whose death she describes in this chapter, the Hubbards have always kept open house—as Ann tried to explain to a carpet salesman who refused to believe that she really needed heavy duty tiles in their sitting room: 'But last year nearly 2,000 people used that room' were the words that finally convinced him!

The house was empty and silent with that intensity of quiet that is so evident in the middle of the night. As I walked from room to room there was an all pervading scent of summer flowers. I remembered, I cried, I prayed over and over again, thanking God for my mother and for the privilege of having been with her at the very end—or should I call it the beginning? For she now walks in Light—no more sunglasses, hats with large floppy brims, drawn curtains or troubled eyes; walks freely—no more walking frames, wheelchair or sticks; in the presence of her Lord where there is fulness of joy— no more tears or misunderstandings, no more pain, for arthritis, cancer and the other bodily humiliations of old age, are all things of the past.

The remaining hours of that night were very special for me. Just before a glorious dawn, I walked in the garden amongst so many flowers that mother had loved. The dawn chorus was just beginning and I walked, bare-foot, on grass that was covered with tiny, dewy cobwebs (ugh! how she had loathed and feared spiders!). That spring I had planted so many of my parents' favourite flowers, in the beds just outside mother's windows so that the perfume could reach into her room as she could no longer walk outside. Sweet peas had grown in exotic profusion for the first time in this garden, phlox, night-scented stock, tobacco, snapdragons, marigolds and many other flowers beloved by old-fashioned cottage gardeners. I gathered a bunch and put them beside a bowl of roses in her room.

My grief was very near the surface, for this was the death of a very old and very much loved mother, but there were so many emotions at work, including, even then, a great sense of relief—not just that she was no longer suffering but that my burdens were being lifted too. It would have been easy to put away that kind of relief, to reject such feelings as 'un-Christian', 'unsuitable' or 'unfilial', but I was clearly aware of them and of course this posed a strange tension: 'Am I glad she is dead?' 'I *can't* be.' 'It doesn't seem right.'

My husband had left, less than twenty-four hours before, to go to the Operation Mobilisation Annual Conference in Belgium, and the boys were also away; our elder son was amongst the many thousands attending the Greenbelt Festival and the younger was climbing in Scotland, so none of them could get home for some time. In fact, we were unable to tell our climber son until three days later, when we went to the station to collect him at the end of the Summer bank holiday weekend.

Sharing grief with my only brother on the day of mother's death helped us both to begin to come to terms with our loss. We talked, we wept, we prayed and we remembered together. But overlaying all of this, were deep regrets.

We were both conscious, that day, of things we wished we'd said or done or, more importantly, things we wished we hadn't said in the heat of the moment, on the occasions when our patience had simply given out. Also, I longed to be able to tell my mother all sorts of things which perhaps we had both taken far too much for granted and didn't often discuss. As she was dying, my arms round her, I had told her how much I loved her, but how often had I said that during the previous half century? Why do we so often wait until it is too late?

When we had talked of death and heaven a few days earlier, she had said, 'I believe I'm dying,' to which I replied, 'Yes, I don't think it will be so very long now' (little realising *how* soon death would come).

'That will be lovely,' said mother. 'I often go to bed so happy because I think, perhaps when I wake up in the morning I shall be in Heaven.' So we looked forward with joy and shared, in anticipation, a little of the sadness of the coming parting. Even now I can weep— several years later—when I am reminded of her extreme infirmity in old age. Recently I was taken completely unawares by an odd little incident. I stopped at a motorway restaurant en route for the West Country at a place where, in better times, she and I used to break our journey on the way to visit my brother and his family. As I stopped the car, I saw an elderly man stooping low so that he could tuck his hand under the elbow of a tiny, ancient lady. It was as though the clock had turned back and I could hear the familiar voice, 'Don't clutch my arm. Just hold me gently under my elbow to steady me.' The problem was that, because she was so small and I fairly tall, I, too, had had to stoop to do this. For my husband and brother, both over six foot three inches, the problem was even more acute, as it was, also, for the four tall grandsons.

Then I thought of all those journeys which had been such marathons for an old lady and all punctuated, at frequent intervals, by stops 'for facilities': incontinence was only one of the many burdens with which she had to live. So again I grieved for the times when I was so busy and in so much of a hurry that I did not exercise real Christian patience; often I must have made her life harder, not easier.

Guilt can start a long time before death. Often people

feel guilty that they have been unable or unwilling to absorb a parent into their home; some feel far more guilty, having provided the home, to discover that the tensions become intolerable—thus leading to seriously fraught relationships that can be very damaging. After death all this comes rolling back. Yes, indeed, there is a sense of deep loss. Following mother's death I longed to share things with her—some piece of news that would only make sense to her, because she alone had known me as a tiny child and right on down through the years. There were old family sayings and jokes as well, for she was not only the last of her generation, but also the last link we had with the nineteenth century.

The Bible is so full of encouragement about the fruits of the Spirit that should be evident in our lives; sadly, when under stress, we frequently fail to manifest—particularly when there are no outsiders present—all the love, joy, peace, patience, goodness, faithfulness and gentleness, not to mention self control, that are so necessary in these close family situations.

'Mother, you really shouldn't talk to Granny like that!' the boys would sometimes say. Oh, I knew I shouldn't—but then, like Paul, I frequently had to grieve about the things I didn't mean to do and still found myself doing. Having aged parents living here, certainly taught me to keep short accounts, since there might never be a tomorrow in which to say sorry. Apologies and forgiveness soon became woven into our daily lives.

In my mother's life, she had coped with many problems. When she was only twelve, her own mother died; two years later, she witnessed the accident in which her next sister had been drowned. Many of her close friends had died during the first world war which had started when she was only seventeen, and she herself had not married until her thirties.

My father had suffered from extreme ill health,

chronic asthma and bronchitis, and had had to retire when only thirty-two. From then on, they had lived from day to day until his death, twenty years later, from a severe stroke.

I can still remember myself, as a little child, feeling very angry at seeing him sitting on a kerbstone in a sea-side town gasping for breath. I hadn't been angry with him but with the people who'd hurried past on the other side. I wanted to shout out, 'He's not drunk—he's got asthma. He's my father—can't someone *help* him!?'

That deep sense of impotence hit me again only recently, on seeing a newspaper photograph of an asth-matic child being rushed to hospital from a plane making an emergency landing in Cornwall. As I looked at the picture, the tears flowed yet again—a hurt still remaining from my father's death so long ago.

My valiant little mother had had to cope through all of this, but her puckish sense of humour and the very deep quality of her faith had somehow seen us all through. Her oldest friends looking back on her childhood, described her as having an ethereal, almost spiritual, quality even then, and yet she also had this absurd and extremely infectious sense of humour to go with it. Many of our friends and relatives still smile as they recall her quaint and memorable sayings that had somehow crept into the folklore of a number of families.

This was the mother of whom my fiancé said, in the early days of our engagement, 'If ever she needs a home, we will have her with us.' Of course, at the time we all hoped she would have many long years in her lovely home in the country, and none of us dreamt that the need would arise so soon.

Less than six months after our marriage, everything was changed by a telephone call telling us that my mother had been found unconscious beside the road one evening in November. She too had had a stroke. So when we returned from France 18 months later, she came to live beside (not with) us in a small flatlet we had made for her in our home. But only five years after that we had another overseas posting, so my brother and his wife undertook to create a self-contained flat for my mother. But these were times of real strain for them, as they already had three children under school age, and my sister-in-law's father, who had multiple sclerosis, was already living with them, too.

However, in her last years, my mother returned to live with us permanently in a specially adapted extension that became known as 'the wing'.

Probably one of the most difficult aspects of caring for one's own mother is the imperceptible change of roles. Gradually I took on the parent role whilst my mother changed to becoming more dependent.

Another sad aspect of old age has to do with change. After a severe stroke, or because of some degenerative disease, there can be subtle, sporadic or even total changes in personality. It was a help to be able to pinpoint such specific causes; all the same this aspect of things had an uncanny way of catching me out! Logical thought was certainly not my mother's strongest point towards the end of her life, and sometimes she and I found ourselves in ridiculous tussles over things that were really not that important anyway.

When a lynch pin is removed, everything around it collapses, and I sometimes wondered what would happen if I didn't cope. How vain that sounds! None of us is really that indispensible, but this was honestly how it felt at times. In spite of the many ups and downs, I really believe that the Holy Spirit was present in our home, giving me the strength to cope with all these daily hassles.

Family meals, for example, became times when I felt I belonged to two quite different worlds, as if I were in the middle of a rapidly rocking seesaw—seeing, on the one hand, the frustrations and constraints laid upon the male members of my family, and yet very aware of the needs of this little old lady, on the other. Things were certainly not always easy.

What could I do when that glazed look came over the eyes of the children as, yet again, Grandmother launched out with, 'Have I ever told you about what happened when . . . ?' No amount of 'Yes, Granny,' could stop the flow that followed, and it was occasionally accompanied, *sotto voce*, by a couple of co-narrators, word for word in perfect time. A sense of humour is an intensely important ingredient in life at any time, but the more so when the pressures are on and one's ability to see the funny side seems to evaporate. So often my husband would say, 'Relax, take it lightly,' and while agreeing in principle, the practice never seemed quite to produce the desired result!

In old age mother frequently described herself as feeling just like a brown paper parcel, wrapped, addressed and ready for the post but waiting and waiting to be collected.

'I wonder *why* the Lord doesn't take me Home?' she sometimes asked with a touch of sadness. In spite of reiterated assurances that we all loved and needed her presence, and that there was obviously work for her to do in God's Kingdom here—by prayer and the spoken word—she found it hard to accept what must at times have seemed like endless waiting.

On one occasion mother thought she was dying; in fact she was extremely ill in the night but decided not to ring for help. She said, 'I knew I was dying, I wasn't afraid and I didn't want to disturb you all.' But her time to leave us had not yet come; and I suggested that, next time, she should ring so that I could be with her—even just to say 'Goodbye!'

Wonderfully, I *was* able to be with her when she died. Death really held no fears for her as she knew Jesus as Saviour and Lord but there was one time of anxiety when she wondered whether she would recognise my father in heaven. Fortunately, she was reassured that we are to be known as we have been known, and that brought serenity.

When friends used to visit, mother often said as they left, 'Goodbye, I hope we shan't meet again.' Their various expressions of amazement or tactful self-control were a delight to observe. Then she would follow this with: 'What I mean is—*here;* I hope that when we meet it will be *there,*' adding, in case they still hadn't grasped it, 'Heaven, I mean: with the Lord.'

One of my particular problems was the way in which people saw me. I was frequently met with, 'I do think you are marvellous the way you care for your mother (and later mother-in-law) so gently and lovingly. I am certain I couldn't do it.' What good would it be to say, 'But it's not *always* like that. You should see us sometimes when there's no one else here. She changes, I change.' It would neither have been kind or loyal to have responded in this way to everyone, but obviously we shared the problems with some who were near to us— not least in order that they might pray into the situation as it really was.

Another sentence which cropped us frequently was: 'You have such a wonderful mother—she is such a delight to visit. Her sense of humour has a sparkle and her faith is so simple and uncomplicated.' All of this was perfectly true, but there was also that 'other side' of 'the wonderful old lady'—for few of us are totally consistent: she was often confused, manipulative and really quite difficult when we were alone with her.

Sometimes I would picture a pillar with my mother sitting on the top of this, and a plaque below, engraved

with the words, 'Wonderful Little Old Lady'; and beside
it a similar plinth on which I was standing, above the
engraving, 'Wonderful Caring Daughter'.

Explaining to everyone that our relationship wasn't
always how it seemed from the outside would have been
ungracious and unprofitable for all concerned, but I am
writing this now because I realise that many of us who
get involved in caring for aged parents can so easily feel
guilty, angry or confused—especially after their deaths.

When undertaking to care for a parent like this, our
first thoughts must inevitably be, 'How can I possibly
cope?' and, 'What will this do to my husband and our
marriage—and how will it affect the children?' We have
to look at such questions objectively and honestly before
embarking on such a project. But even then only hind-
sight can effectively answer these questions, and this can
quickly land us back in the 'if only' syndrome: 'If only we
hadn't had mother here.' 'If only she had remained well.'
'If only the tensions between the generations had never
occurred.'

Inevitably much of this is uppermost in our thinking at
the time of bereavement, and the sorrow and loss become intermingled with whispers of false guilt with
which the devil loves to burden us, leaving us confused
and hurt. Mercifully, both the good and the bad memories can be brought to the surface, faced and dealt with in
the light of that much-quoted verse from the first chapter
of John: 'If we claim to be without sin we deceive ourselves and the truth is not in us. If we confess our sins he
is faithful and just and will forgive our sins and cleanse us
from all unrighteousness.'

For some months following my mother's death, I used
to spend time imagining conversations that I wished I
could have had with her. Many who care for an aged
parent will find that there are regrets like this, but it must
be recognised that death is not the end of a chapter—

instead a whole new book has been opened. The believing loved one has already gone on ahead to a wonderful new life, where our regrets can change nothing—and are not even needed!

If one scans the death columns of the national papers it becomes clear that there are increasing numbers of four generation families today. The phrase, 'Beloved mother, grandmother, and great grandmother,' tells its own story. People today live much longer, but where and how are they going to live? It's clear that most geriatric hospitals are full to bursting, whilst new nursing homes and residential homes for the elderly are opening every month. Sheltered housing proliferates and yet there still aren't enough places for those who need them. So much of the Bible teaching is about loving and caring for each other, that we are now being encouraged to look again at the role of the extended family, by organisations such as the Jubilee Centre.

However, whilst there are some families who can easily absorb ageing parents, there are clearly others for whom this is an impossibility. Before we enter into these far-reaching decisions, there has to be a great deal of honest discussion and prayer about the implications, so that we truly believe we are doing the best for all concerned. Then, when our parents eventually leave us, we can look back and remind ourselves of how we reached those decisions.

The longer our parents survive, the more time we have for really knowing them. Maybe that seems an obvious enough statement, but it helps to explain why, for many, the grief of an aged parent's death is such a deeply-felt experience. Looking forward to a reunion in heaven certainly tempers the sense of loss, but can never completely alleviate it.

Soon after my mother's death, I had to have a hip replacement operation which gave me a completely new lease of life. I was suddenly relieved from the nagging pain of the past, and found that I was once more able to walk with pleasure and tackle the heavier jobs in the garden which I so much enjoyed. It was a wonderful relief.

But then another mother arrived.

My husband's mother who had so repeatedly emphasised that she would never live with us, and never allow herself to become a burden, suddenly found herself in circumstances which dictated urgent action. She had been wonderfully cared for, for over twenty-five years, by a much-loved housekeeper and companion, who was no longer able to cope because of increasing age and very serious back trouble. So, for a short time, they both came to live with us. Whilst it was understood that this was to be a temporary arrangement, we had had little time beforehand to discuss the pros and cons of this quite different situation.

For much of her life my mother-in-law had had an unusually large number of health problems, and needed much love and care. In addition, many in the wider family had, in the past, voiced the opinion that it would not be wise for her to live with us. At any rate, we were determined that any decision should be made by all of us.

The boys, then aged twenty-one and eighteen, were very concerned as to how this new arrangement would affect us—particularly for my husband's sake, since he was the only child and there could, in this case, be no shared responsibility.

Eventually we reached a common agreement that my mother-in-law should come to live with us, but that there should be regular breaks built into the programme so that we could all have 'space'—physical, emotional and mental. This was provided by occasional visits to a nursing home.

My mother-in-law had had an interesting and varied life and I loved to listen, notebook in hand, whilst she reminisced. There were so many things that could only be conveyed first-hand—memories of the opening days of this century shared in anecdotes and stories, as well as the wisdom gained in a life spanning eighty-five years. She had a strong and interesting character, and a considerable talent as a water-colourist.

To honour our parents is the first commandment, accompanied by a promise. Caring for an old parent undoubtedly puts great demands on us, but it can also enrich. As we watched the body prisons being left behind, we were able to join in the old people's happiness that they would soon have brand new bodies.

Not long before my husband's mother died, a retired missionary visited her, whilst she was reading from her beautiful large print Bible.

'It's Revelation, but I'm not sure I understand it,' she said.

'That doesn't matter,' her friend replied, 'as long as our names are written in the Lamb's Book of Life.'

'Oh yes,' came the firm reply.

And whilst we ourselves mourn the loss of their physical presence, we can be glad because we know that their names are written in that Book.

When sorting through my mother's books one day, I discovered a tiny piece of paper on which were printed words from John's third letter: 'I have no greater joy than to hear that my children are walking in the truth.' Surely that must be the heartfelt prayer of every Christian parent and grandparent.

Elisabeth Casson was brought up by missionary parents in Africa where she experienced not only the very real presence of God and the power of evil, but also the inevitability of death.

It was here that she first met her husband James, whose premature death she writes about in this chapter. It was not until they were both qualified—he as a doctor and she a physiotherapist, that they were married almost six years later.

James had always wanted to serve the Lord overseas, so, after several house jobs in England, they went to Tanzania with their two small children to work in the Kilimanjaro Christian Medical Centre as CMS associates. Being nomadic made them very reliant on the Lord, and on other friends and family for their support and shelter.

They eventually returned to Chipping Sodbury where James became a GP, and it was here that, soon after they had settled down and made a home for themselves, they discovered that James would not be with the family for much longer. However, the Lord assured the family of his ability to care for them in matters large and small, and he has never let them down.

Elisabeth worked as a part-time physiotherapist, thus allowing her time to be available to the children as they were growing up. They are now moving on to higher education. Together they wait for 'the new thing' promised in Isaiah chapter 43 verse 10: 'But the Lord says, "Do not cling to the events of the past or dwell on what has happened long ago. Watch for the new thing I am going to do. It is happening already—you can see it now."'

It is easy to talk about James—he was vibrant, totally involved in all he did—and always busy. He was the one in our partnership who kept everything going, made the decisions and had the ideas; he was the one most hard hit by the realisation that his life was about to end.

It all started when he had a biopsy done for a bleeding mole. At first I didn't grasp the implications of this, but I gathered that he was worried. It was a terrible blow when the GP walked in and asked me to join him to tell James that the result of the biopsy was malignant. James thought he was talking about someone else. When the GP left, we prayed, without saying much to each other, but asking the Lord to take the situation into his hands. We felt like two children on a raft in the middle of the ocean.

A hospital admission was arranged, and it seemed as if everything was in control, but we were locked into our own griefs. During the day things went on as usual, but night times were different. Often I just cried through the night.

The lesson the following Sunday was about Abraham offering his only son Isaac, the one for whom all the promises had been made, to God as a sacrifice. It occurred to me then that just as Isaac was a gift from God to Abraham, so James was a gift from God to me, to love and to enjoy—and now it seemed as if God was asking for him back. This insight was a tremendous relief to me, and a very positive directive to love and enjoy James while he was still loaned to me. I was given a deep peace, as well as a heightened enjoyment of James, for eighteen months. This, rather than making separation more difficult, actually made it easier somehow.

It took James a year to find his answer to, 'Why me?' When he saw the number of people going for radiotherapy he realised that the question wasn't 'Why me?' but, 'Why not me?' Initially his reaction to the prognosis was to realise that his spiritual life wasn't up to standard. He had been very busy and various things had slipped. He spent the ten days before his hospital admission sorting out his priorities with the Lord. He didn't want to die; in fact he felt that he was just beginning to live. However he was grateful for this jolt to help him sort out his life and get things into perspective. I realised that James had some tremendous spiritual experiences during his stay in hosptial but he wasn't able to be coherent about them. It was enough for me just to know that he had been strengthened and encouraged by the Lord. In fact it was as if he had had a conversion experience all over again.

After his death, I found a tape with an attempt to tell his dreams. He did admit that he was given a particularly hallucinatory type of anaesthetic, but still the dreams were very real for him. They were important because they changed his idea of heaven and showed him something very helpful about the purpose of life. Actually, before this James hadn't wanted to go to heaven at all. He had thought it was a 'goody goody' sort of place where people sat around doing nothing or playing harps; and, being a very active sort of person, that didn't interest him very much. In one dream he was taken up out of the world and beyond, through steps of time, to the gates of heaven. Standing there were two people, one he recognised and one whom he'd never met, but both were people who had played a formative role in his Christian life. They welcomed him and as he talked to them, he looked beyond into heaven and saw a wonderful sight. Everything in heaven was what his soul longed for. He saw total fulfilment and purpose, a completeness and a meaningfulness with the Lord; in fact a place that was total delight, and he wanted to be there. He made as if to enter, but a hand was put round his shoulder and he was turned round and told to go back. He believed then that he had been healed, even when he had secondaries, because he hadn't been allowed to enter then but had been given the commission to go back. Later he realised, through thinking about the next dream, that it wasn't the length of one's life that was important but to whom you belong and whom you serve. One thing was certain: heaven was where he now wanted to go. His eyes were set ahead.

In his second dream, as he climbed up through years of time into space, the world shrank. He could see it getting smaller and smaller until it looked like a stage. He could see all the actions in the whole world at once. There were all sorts of people on this world-stage—rich and poor, old and young, hungry and fat, illiterate and clever—going around engaged in their normal activities. There seemed to be no plot or purpose to the play except that some people came off after only a small part, while others had comparatively long parts to play. Then he saw the important point of the play: the side on which the actors went off. Those who belonged to Christ went off on one side and those who did not, went off on the other. Suddenly many spiritual problems came into perspective for James. To share Christ became all important, not the length of his life.

The dreams didn't end the struggle although they gave

him a great deal of help. He understood that the Lord wanted him, totally, and likened this experience to a tube of toothpaste being squeezed until finally there was nothing left in the tube.

During the last six months of his life, there were two main areas of conflict. The first was whether to accept the healing ministry of his friends. If he didn't, it implied either that he wasn't trying to get better or that he didn't believe that God would make him better. If he did, it would expose him to a completely new field of experience about which, as a scientist and a conventional churchman, he was uncertain. He believed that God could heal him—in fact, for a time he believed that God *had* healed him—but now, with well-established secondaries, it was difficult to see what he should do. The struggle was fierce; another squeeze of the toothpaste as he said, 'Thy will be done,' and stepped into the unknown with the Lord.

The whole matter was wonderfullly taken care of. A friend and priest, whom he hadn't seen for years, came to visit him. He prayed over him, naming each symptom, and anointing and laying hands on him after a time of confession. Another friend took him to a healing fellowship in Bristol where he found new joy and tremendous support. In fact some of these members came every week to our home just to support us in prayer. We experienced such peace as a result of these sessions, during which they simply upheld us in prayer and quietly left afterwards. James was healed of many distressing symptoms, such as his bad dreams and constant vomiting, for which he was very grateful. He had a new peacefulness, too; but the lumps on his body continued to appear and grow.

The second problem is one which many people have to face: that of suffering. James broke his arm about six months before he died. It was difficult for him to do much. He was too weak to stand for long and he couldn't sit much either. It was easy to feel down and wonder why God allowed him to suffer. Wasn't it enough that he was going to die? Why make him suffer in this way as well? Doubts about the goodness of God, about his love and his kindness, mounted up. I had no answers. It was bad enough to know that James had a lot of discomfort whatever his position, without this mental stress as well.

The nights were often disturbed and scripture offered no comfort, until one night, the realisation came that God wasn't just passively watching James suffer; he was suffering too, as he had suffered when he had watched Jesus. God hadn't intervened when Christ had suffered but had stood by him, strengthening him, supporting him and suffering with him. Then James knew that God was with him in an evil world, waiting for the end and certain victory: another spiritual battle won; another squeeze of the toothpaste tube.

What is it like to die? Many people wonder about this. The trouble is that none of us knows; most people seem to fear the actual dying process. The problem is that we don't actually know when it's going to happen. This puts quite a strain on the person who is dying, but possibly more so on the loved ones who often fear walking in unexpectedly on death.

Some evenings, four or five months before James died, he sometimes said, 'I feel so awful tonight, I think I'm going to die. No, I can't die tonight: I've got such and such to do tomorrow.' The will to live was very strong although he was ready to die and was looking forward to the 'celestial city'. Latterly, he anticipated death peacefully, knowing that it was coming and that everything was ready. In the meantime we were prepared to enjoy the present. I found it difficult to get used to simply experiencing the moments of being together and not necessarily doing anything at all. The snag was that there was an awful lot do to: housework, the garden, looking after the children and so on. I'm sure we should be ready for the Lord's return in a similar way. In spite of the hours I spent with James, these other duties were up-to-date and in order because the Lord had them in control.

How do you talk to someone about dying? They don't necessarily want to talk about dying with someone emotionally close. They might even prefer to talk about dying with someone they hardly know at all; to talk about it with you, or someone else they know well, may be emotionally stressful: one of you might break down; and that's something neither would want to risk. Alternatively, the relative might not want to make you sad and so avoids talking about death. In James's case, he was an optimist. He didn't expect to die, even when he had well-developed secondaries.

James liked planning, so we had talked about finance and made plans for the future. However, it hit me hard when he started talking about repaying our small mortgage. He hadn't resigned his hospital appointment either, and I wondered if he had really come to terms with death. A strange situation seems to arise when someone has accepted and looks forward to death, only to put it behind him and get on with the present task of living, seemingly secure about the future. In this atmosphere I found planning very difficult until I realised that if it was right to go ahead with a course of action, it was right whether James lived or died. There weren't two rights, one if he should live, and the other if he should die.

It was strange, too, that although James totally accepted the Lord's forgiveness, he saw the egg-like lumps which appeared on his body as a penance or something to be put up with as a reminder of how abhorrent our sin is to God. He still felt himself to be unsightly and didn't wish to be touched. This I found distressing. I had to content myself with loving nursing rather than giving or receiving a cuddle. But, as his lumpy body wasted away, a beautiful spiritual transformation took place: he glowed.

I slept better if I didn't share a bed with James but I did want to be in the same room as him; just to be there if he died, rather than to walk in and find him dead. More practically, I wanted to be there during the long hours of the night just to talk to him, to read, to get a drink or some medication, often three or four times a night. He was always sorry to disturb me but I was glad to be there, especially latterly when he couldn't do things for himself. What amazed me was that I could get up several times in the night and drop into a deep sleep on returning to bed: a great blessing.

To go back to the question of the physical act of dying —James was frightened about this. He had seen people die badly and in distress, and he wondered how he would perform. That apart, there was the guilt of feeling that, as a Christian, he shouldn't be afraid of dying. Yes, he was looking forward to going to be with the Lord, so why was he worried about dying? We discussed this several times and then we remembered Christian's reluctance, in *Pilgrim's Progress,* to swim across the river, although he could see the celestial city, and although the angel had said he would look after him as he was swimming. Then we realised that in each of us there is a deep survival instinct, the instinct to fight death and to live at all costs; and that there is no need to feel guilty about living and wanting to live.

When the time came, on his last evening, James felt so well that he didn't wish for his injection of Diamorphine which he had been having for the previous three days. We had a usual sort of night but the next day he felt terribly tired. I said I'd wash him while he woke up. He chatted a little, saying how glad he was that I could manage to look after him at home, and then sleep got the better of him. Only when I had finished, did I realise that, in fact, he had drifted into unconsciousness. Some hours later, his pulse stopped. He had died. His worst fears were over. He had just slipped from life, through death, to life; no knock-out drugs, no distress, just a peaceful slipping away. He looked forward to heaven, remembering his dreams. He had also looked forward to a new body with no lumps on it and no pain. In fact, he had had a very poor body image; something, I know, that quite a number of people with all kinds of disability have. There had been, he had thought, nothing beautiful about his body covered in lumps and he hadn't felt that anybody would want to touch something so distasteful. For him, heaven with a new body was quite something!

When James first heard he had cancer, he didn't know who to share the news with. He didn't want everybody to know. He didn't want to tell the children. He didn't want the patients in the practice to know, in case new people felt reluctant to join the practice. James told his parents after his first operation, when he felt he was already on his way to recovery, although to be in hospital over Christmas does make things seem urgent. Presuming all was well, not wanting the children to hear rumours, or the patients to be upset, we kept quiet. Inevitably, friends and relatives got to know, but people were most discreet. When to tell the children became a nagging problem for me, as the secondaries became more generalised and the prognosis a reality. One day, a close friend said that she had heard a rumour that James had cancer. She wondered whether Rosie, our daughter, knew the nature of James's illness and suggested that she be told before she heard it from an outsider and felt let down by us.

The time had come. When Rosie came back from

school, I told her straight away, leaving time to chat it over long before bedtime. I simply told her that various people were talking about her Dad's illness, and I wanted her to know that the illness was cancer, and that he wasn't recovering in the way we had hoped and expected. Like many another child, she made a non-committal comment and went off. I was the one who was surprised; I had expected tears and a great many questions. The relief was tremendous, tinged with a little guilt at not having discussed it first with James. Later, after I had told Peter, our son, James asked me if Rosie knew, and was relieved to hear that she had been told. Both of us found it agonising trying to decide how much (and how) to tell the children.

Sometimes the children asked if Dad was going to get better. (Of course, we prayed that he would.) My answer was that I hoped so; but, although God had taken away some of the distressing symptoms, Dad was getting weaker. On several occasions we were able to talk about James belonging to God and about the fact that at some time or another, those who believe in Jesus go to be with him in heaven. It might be soon for James; but, if God were to take James early, then he would have a special responsibility to look after us. We talked about ways in which he had done this already and therefore we could trust him to do so in the future.

Having evening prayers together gave us very special opportunities to talk about our hopes and fears. One day Rosie's worst fear happened. Two children were chatting over the dinner table at school. In Rosie's hearing one child said, 'Did you know Rosie's Dad's got cancer?' Rosie flinched, waiting for all the questions to come, but they went on talking as if it was the most ordinary thing to have said. She realised then that her friends had no idea of the implications of cancer.

During the last three months it became widely known

that James had cancer and Rosie felt that she had to talk about this with a friend, though she was reluctant to do so. Mostly, she was busy with club activities and the neighbours' dog, which all helped to occupy her. Home isn't exactly a happy place to be when there is someone terminally ill there. To be honest, I think Rosie found it distressing to be with James and so, after an exchange of greetings and chat, she would tactfully find other things to do. James found he couldn't climb the stairs, so for the last six weeks he opted to stay upstairs on our very comfortable bed. It was at this stage that Rosie became used to James being around, but not present at meals; so after he had died, for quite some time, she had the feeling that he was still around.

The day James died, Rosie providentially had after-school activities which kept her away until the very moment he slipped away. I heard her coming in and asked her to pop in to see Dad. Just holding his hand, which of course was warm, I said that he had drifted from sleep into death. The timing was perfect. I am sure that sharing in James's illness, talking about it, and then seeing him at that moment when he had just died, helped Rosie to talk naturally about James, and our experiences with him, soon after his death.

Our son, Peter, however, who was a little older than Rosie, was a quiet and kind eleven year old, away at boarding school. His friend's father had died of cancer: he knew what the score could be. We kept Peter posted about the different operations and the fact that James was carrying on at work, but when Peter came home before the second Christmas to find Dad going in to hospital again, he was very fed up. Then he suddenly said to me, 'Anyway, what's the matter with Dad?' It was late in the first evening of the holidays: not the best moment to tackle such a topic. We had a stormy session. Peter knew about cancer and had seen his father getting weaker. We sat and cried together. He kept repeating, 'I love Daddy.' He settled down, finally, that night. The next day I took him in to the hospital to see James before his operation, just to say how much he loved him.

By the Easter holidays, James could only walk unsteadily for a few yards. He looked emaciated. Peter found this extremely distressing. He wanted to be with James, but it was difficult to bear it. A few days before James died, he wrote to Peter. He felt that this would be the last time that he would write, 'I feel so ill.' This letter arrived the day he died, so, when I turned up at the school to see Peter, he knew what had happened. I was glad to be able to tell him the news in person but he didn't want to talk about James's death or to hear how it had happened. That was all right by me.

It took Peter quite a long time to feel that he could talk about James and remember the happy times we had had together. There were some advantages in having been away at boarding school; but not having had to live with dying seemed to make it more difficult for him to talk about James afterwards.

A question people often ask me is, 'How did the children come to terms with James's death?' I've never asked them; it just seems like an analytically adult question. Primarily, children get on with living. One day I hope they will tell me the answer to that question. In the meantime, I've tried to share the encouragement the Lord has graciously given to me, and I hope that my trust and confidence in him will have a stabilising influence on them to enable them to do their own adjusting; because, ultimately, people have to come to accept another person's suffering in their own way and to find their own answers.

My own personal problem was when and how much to help James. This was particularly highlighted when he broke his arm. He wasn't used to being unable to use part of his body. His arm was in a long plaster bent at the elbow—not very manageable. I wanted to help him, knowing that in a day or two he would be used to the plaster and independent; but he wouldn't have any of that. To stand by watching someone struggling when you can help, is frustrating. I felt hurt to have my assistance spurned and yet amazed to see James so motivated to keep going. He learnt to write well with his left hand and could use a screw-driver; his ununited fracture was just ignored.

I think it needs stressing that the attendant needs almost as much support as the person who is ill, if the demands are heavy or continual. Gradually friends stop visiting: they don't know what to say or are embarrassed by the progressive illness. One becomes increasingly isolated. Even a quick trip out is a welcome relief, but all the time one is worried about what is happening at home. I was fortunate in having a friend who called regularly and unobtrusively; if it wasn't convenient for her to see James, she would chat to me. One day I realised how much I valued the attention she gave to me. Everyone else visited James; she encouraged me, advising me on nursing aids and leaving without making any demands on my time or energy. Latterly, she sat in for me while I went shopping. She was content to sit in an adjacent room so that James did not have to exhaust himself being sociable. It was wonderful to have such a supportive and unobtrusive visitor.

I hadn't been asked directly by anyone, or should I say I hadn't answered honestly, the question, 'What does it feel like to live with someone who is dying?' I am inclined to shy off, to talk about *James's* experiences, but in this account I have tried to be a little more honest about my own. I have valued this time to sit down, not just to think about how James came to terms with his own illness but also to look back and see how I myself have come to terms with it: the difficulties and the joys. Looking back, I know I have grown spiritually, that I have experienced God's power in a new and wonderful way. I wouldn't wish that any of these experiences were taken away from me, but it would be wonderful if James were here too.

At first it was difficult to believe that he was not upstairs. We laid for him at table and offered to take drinks up to him. It was as if he was still with us. We 'knew' that he was not there, but we felt that he was very close—a feeling that persisted. It was as if he had gone on a journey for some months and I had been left to take responsibility until he returned. I was used to that. Also, all the major decisions had been made; it was two years before I really had to make one of my own. I felt as if I was in limbo. I was grateful for this, since I had personal matters to sort out and I needed the time to do this.

In spite of being able to manage, I had always looked to James for support and encouragement. For several months he had been physically unable to do much, but he could and did tell me exactly what to do: where to drill, for example, or which drill bit or which size Rawl plug to use, so that between us we could hang up the curtain rail. Now he was no longer there to give the instructions and encouragement or to make the decisions. In a very real sense, I was only a half of the partnership which had matured over twelve years. Incompleteness in every aspect of my life was more acute for me than loneliness.

This partnership severance, this loss of a friend and ally, left me bereft and bewildered. Not only had I lost my supporter but I was also left wondering, 'Who am I?' This had been quite clear when James had been alive: we had been well known as GP and wife, following, a little uncomfortably, in James's parents' footsteps. Our roles had been well defined. Now I was no longer a GP's wife so where was my place?

Three months after James' death, I went to Nairobi to help my mother leave hospital and return to England. While there, I was my mother's child: everyone knew me as a Ridsdale, not a Casson. I was referred to in that way. It was as if I had had no children and had never been married. This led to an identity crisis: Who was I? Whose name should I use? Fortunately, because I had to take some responsibility for my mother, and because we went our separate ways on returning to England, I did not become the child again. Once back home, it was natural to be a Casson and easier for the children. My name became unimportant but the underlying question remained. I was no longer married to James, I was on my own and had an identity of my own to take up.

Some people, during the following year, invited me to take part in various functions because James and I had attended them together previously. That was kind, but until I had finished playing the GP's wife it was difficult to start again. My position in the community was due to James being a GP; our lifestyle was connected to his salary. Now I had neither the position nor the salary.

I am not sure when I realised that finance is a great leveller. The best advice I had, came from my brother who, casually over the phone, explained that my pensions were my income and that I had to live on them and not on my assets, adding, 'Set your living standard to your income, girl.' The harsh reality of finding my identity was not made easier by the niggling concern as to whether I could manage on my pensions, but my changing situation was smoothed considerably by the fact that I lived in a large and interesting house and was used to a simple lifestyle.

Three years later, the Lord organised a house-move for us. I had not anticipated the effect it would have on us. The village was very close to where we had been living, but we came as new people, without a history, having to find our own place, and we were accepted as newcomers. Few people even knew James. However, very soon we were on Christian name terms, accepted as we were. However, I am aware of and grateful to those around who are concerned for our welfare and who have provided a sense of security and continuity to our lives. This sense of belonging would have been lost if we had moved further away.

Six years later there is still a gap, a sense of loss, but I feel whole—not amputated—as a person again. God has kept his assurance to us that if he took James away he would indeed be with us instead. I am aware of the danger of trusting in my own strength, and so when I feel weak, then I turn to God. It is better to remain inadequate in myself and close to God than to be rehabilitated and to discard him.

While driving James back from a service in Bristol one night, the car broke down. Neither of us knew anything at all about cars. James felt angry and helpless because he was too tired and weak to get out of the car, so I had to. I opened the bonnet, saw some loose wires and, in spite of having no equipment and being frozen stiff, attached them to a likely place. The car started and we burst into tears—aware of the Lord's closeness to us then, and confident that his help would be available in similar situations for me in the future. Three years later, I bought a new car, expecting trouble-free driving. This has not been the case but the Lord has always been there sending his assistance in many different disguises. In a letter James wrote from hospital, he said, 'I don't know what the next year will hold, but I do know that the One who may call me to take a special short cut up a narrow steep path to the mountain summit, is going to look after you in a very special way as you follow the more gentle gradient to the same place.' Those words have proved true.

Bereavement, as I see it, is a sense of loss, the absence —in some cases—of someone who has become not just a part of oneself but one's whole way of life. Grief is the expression of the emotions associated with that loss. I always thought I had grieved with James while he was ill and as he died, so that all I would have to do would be to get on with the job of living without him. Looking back now, I can see that I was numb for several months without realising it. Fortunately the daily routines and special demands, such as the funeral, were there, which all helped to carry me along.

James and I had planned a summer holiday knowing that he would probably not be there. I was reluctant to take this, unsure about how I would manage the drive, the memories and any organising that would need doing. The children really looked forward to going back to a familiar place with a family they enjoyed being with. That family stood by us, sharing our memories of previous holidays of which they were not a part and took all responsibility for making it an enjoyable time. I just went along with it all, 'carried' by dear friends.

Looking around, I realised how many 'uncles' the children had. I remember saying to Peter that although we had lost James, God had given him plenty of 'uncles' to stand by him. They might be second-best in his eyes, but like an artificial limb to an amputee, these 'uncles' could be very good substitutes. Our extended family and godparents are among those who have stood behind us: a great blessing. I used to feel particularly on my own at weekends; it was then that we would go visiting, the families to which we turned filled the gaps.

Somehow I managed the endless official letters and paperwork. There seemed to be plenty of time for everything in those early lifeless days. One problem was how to deal with the tax forms. I hit on the idea of just doing

one item a day and not worrying about the magnitude of
the task: a step at a time. A friend sent me a card with
this thought on it: 'If you look at the sun you won't see
the shadows.' So I plodded along, trying to do this. I did
not cry or get angry in those days, I was serene and
lifeless. I had to keep my eyes upwards; I knew I could
not manage if I looked around. I am not sure how long I
stayed numb or what triggered the first outburst. But one
day I found myself standing at the French windows looking down the garden with tears running down my face,
weeping angrily at my ineptitude and sorry for myself at
having to manage on my own. I regret that these out-
bursts happened fairly often after that, but I felt that
there was no one to run to for help. The right sort of help
never seemed quite available when I needed it, so ultimately there I was on my own. There seemed to be only
two options: either to stand up and face the situation
and, with God's help, get on with it, or to collapse. I
chose the former.

Most of the time, I have been overwhelmed by God's
ample provision; this has left me with little room for self-
pity. When I lost some money in a firm which went bank-
rupt instead of allowing me to wallow in self pity, the
Lord sent me someone who needed a little support after
she had lost everything in a bankruptcy. It was good to
come back to life again, even if it did mean experiencing
anger, tears and the feelings of loneliness.

James and I had not lived in the area long. An old
house, a new job, as well as church and community
meetings had kept us busy. We had not had much time
or felt the need to make new friends. His illness, and the
work that it entailed, actually caused some contacts to
drop away. His death and the awkwardness of not knowing what to say to me, caused others to do the same. I
found that I had very few close friends although there
were many who were willing to be friendly. I was the one

who kept them away, often, by presenting a competent, self-sufficient front. This was a shallow veneer over my helplessness and lack of confidence. My daughter pointed out one day that she was certain most people didn't realise I was a widow. She felt I managed too well. She gets cross when people ask me to help out when there are others around who do not have to look after house, garden, go to work and look after the family on their own. She feels I should be the one applying for help.

I am ambivalent in the way I see our family. Most of the time I feel ours is quite a normal one—apart from the gap James has left. This gap is not usually exposed except on parents' evenings at school or family occasions, such as Christmas, or when I am invited to friends for the evening and all the others are in pairs. The children are used to our complete/incomplete family and often call me Mama-Papa. If I seemed less able to manage, I expect I would have more friends and more support, so this air of normality and competence has both its advantages and disadvantages.

Is it a delusion or a safe-guard against a stereotype that prevents me thinking of our family as a single-parent family? After six years of life without James, am I deluding myself in not accepting that I am single? I had, like most widows, continued to wear a wedding ring—it made it easier at school functions—but was I hiding behind it? Certainly, wearing the ring on another finger —as I did later on—was significant. This single act of transferring a ring represented a tremendous struggle during which I not only accepted my singleness but also the possibility that people would think I was divorced rather than widowed. Perhaps only now I am coming to terms with my bereavement and accepting my loss. I still weep for James: no longer tears of grief or despair, but tears of love. I also have to remind myself that I am not the only one who misses him.

As a young widow, I should, perhaps, say something about re-marriage. One of the saddest but most lovely moments James and I had, was when he had told me how much he loved me and therefore—though he could hardly say this—wanted me to feel free to re-marry. I was taken by surprise: the thought had not crossed my mind. I would have married *him* again, given the chance, but it was just like him not only to think of the possibility of my marrying someone else, but also to plan to make it easier for me. Since then I have wondered whether I should re-marry for the sake of the children or for companionship, but the readjustment would—it seems to me—be enormous.

A few months after James had died, I realised that someone was interested in me, but this was too soon after my loss and I was still unused to getting out and about on my own; nor had I settled my affairs. Fortunately, we both decided that we had divergent interests and parted.

Twelve years of marriage had left me feeling like a teenager, as I realised when another man asked me out for a meal. I was quite unused to being dated and found it emotionally unsettling. Moving house at the same time added to the conflicts, but the person concerned was a godsend: really reliable and supportive during a very disturbing time, he helped me to come back to life emotionally. Then I stopped seeing him. He had helped me so much: had I just used him? I wasn't sure, but I hoped not.

Then came *my* chance to help someone else. We both had 'gaps': he was divorced and I was a widow. We enjoyed going out together and exchanging ideas. I realised that my bereavement was not so different from his divorce. Both of us had to grieve for our losses and learn the skills of our partners in order to get our lives together again. My experiences were being useful to someone else and were enabling me to understand another person better.

In my work as a community physiotherapist, there have been many times when I have been able to empathise with my patients who have also been recently bereaved. Two factors have assisted me in particular.

Elderly widows often say to me, 'But you've got the children.' That is true. The children have not only been a comfort and support to me but have also motivated me to keep going, cook meals and go out. Many widows I know live on their own; sometimes no one calls all day; and they have little inclination to prepare a meal for themselves.

Undoubtably, the other key factor for me was the insight I was given when we first heard of James' cancer: that James and the children were given to me as a gift from God to be looked after and enjoyed for as long as they lived. The Lord took James to be with him and left me the children. James and I both understood that the purpose of life was that we should come to believe in Jesus and that any extra time granted to us subsequently was a bonus in which to serve him, until our turn came to be called into God's presence. This certainty helped me to let go of James, and give him back to the Lord, trusting that he would faithfully guide and help us who are left behind as we continue to serve him, until the day when we, too, will be called into God's glorious presence.

10   **Dying – the Greatest**   *James Casson*
         Adventure of My Life

This chapter is different from the previous ones in that
James Casson, a young GP, wrote it as one facing and
coping not with someone else's dying and death but with
his own. It was first published by Christian Medical
Fellowship Publications as a booklet, and is reproduced
here, suitably edited, with permission.

At the beginning of Chapter 9, there are brief bio-
graphical details of James' life with Elisabeth. He wrote
the unique material which follows in the last months of
his life, before his death in June 1980.

This chapter is written not only for those who suffer, though they may choose to glance through it, but also for those who look after them, particularly at home. It has not been easy to write. One reason for this is because it has meant some necessary self-examination, whereas it is important for any sufferer from terminal or incurable illness to have his mind directed away from himself. His thoughts should be outwards to what is happening around him or towards the Christian proclamation that death is but the beginning of something far greater.

Speaking both as a doctor and patient, I confess that it is only now that I am aware of my own great limitations as a doctor. The experience has been a humbling one in this respect, as much as in any other.

Certainly the experience of dying is more difficult than I had expected.

The problems of terminal cancer begin on the day when the original treated condition is found to be still active, long before the patient is sufficiently ill to require weekly or daily visits from his doctor. Life for both the patient and his immediate family is never quite the same thereafter. For this reason I make no apology for the inclusion of the section on the Christian hope.

Dying makes life suddenly real. Watching my slow physical deterioration reaffirmed my belief that there is something else within which will survive, because, if for no other reason my personality stayed the same in spite of the eroding bodily form in which it was confined. Slowly I have come to terms in my own way with my own circumstances; each must find his own way to resolve his own conflict. Unfortunately, the oft-quoted remark by tearful relatives, 'He was such a wonderful man, doctor,' is never really true; and if the survival of the spirit after death were to depend on the quality of our earthly life, a moment's reflection would show that our chances are small.

There is no doubt that Christian teaching emphasises that God can always produce good out of any situation if we will let him. For this reason, the most tragic and desperate circumstances in human experience can be turned to good. Even if you are not normally a religious person, I would ask you to read the section on the Christian hope, as it may help you to find the road to faith. Certainly the practical matters raised in the next section will be of benefit in the many adjustments which are demanded by terminal illness, both for the patient and those who look after him.

Finally may I emphasise that nothing I have written is meant to imply criticism of the many friends and relatives who have supported me through my terminal illness —which has been the greatest adventure of my life.

PRACTICAL PROBLEMS

I thought I was alone in having to face one particular problem until I overheard a conversation while I was waiting in a queue for radiotherapy. One patient turned to another and said, 'You know, I haven't been out of the house since Christmas.'

'Why not?'

'Oh, I never know what to say to people when they

keep asking me how I'm getting on.'

She went on to say that when in hospital, she had received ninety get well cards.

I am sure such problems and others—which I identify and comment on below—will be shared by many.

How are you?

There is no answer to such a question. People all mean well, but to answer the traditional English greeting, 'How are you?' when you feel tired, distended, full of general discomfort and know that you are suffering from a terminal illness, is almost impossible. To say how you really feel brings stunned embarrassment. The best suggestion I can offer is that you offer a different greeting like, 'Good morning. Nice to see you out,' and a comment about the weather.

Telephone calls

By all means phone for news but bear in mind that you may be the third caller that evening and be prepared for the news not always to be good. Again rephrase the question perhaps to, 'What sort of day has X had?' Please do not expect the sick person to answer the call— it is very difficult to say the same things over and over again, particularly if one is feeling awful. Somehow I felt I was letting the caller down if I said how ill I was feeling.

Letters

A brief comment such as, 'Please don't bother to reply to this letter,' will make all the difference to the conscience of the recipient. Again it is all to do with our custom of answering letters—quite unintentionally, you may be burdening the patient, rather than sharing the distress and showing your concern for his welfare.

At this point one has to ask how you should keep in touch. Flowers are always appreciated and fruit usually so. Peppermint creams seem to help hyperacidity and reflux. It may help to have a friendly relative or neighbour who is kept fully informed and who can help the spouse of the patient in telling well-wishers what is happening.

Visitors

Once they had arrived, I was always pleased to see them. The golden rule is not to stay too long, even if the patient appears to be bright and alert. It is afterwards that he will get so tired. The prospect of endless visitors can be rather daunting. At one stage my wife and I always began the day by seeing who was coming. Also, it is sometimes difficult to feel gracious towards people who often invited over but always replying that it was too far to come, suddenly all turn up without the slightest problem. I felt rather conscious that they were all looking in before 'the old chap snuffed it'. These type of thoughts usually assailed me before people arrived however; and I enjoyed meeting relatives and old friends almost more than anything else, during the earlier and intermediate stage of my condition; if I was in significant pain or under strong drugs, my reactions would be different.

Here are several further thoughts for visitors. First, do not be too effusive and jocular to start with. We patients are subject to mood swings and a hail and hearty approach will be quite acceptable one day but extremely irritating the next. Second, be careful before bringing books and magazines to lend. Many visitors brought along 'just a couple of books you might enjoy'. This was well meant, but I quietly accumulated a dozen books a week. One does not want to upset anyone by not reading their particular gem, but it becomes impossible to read them all. The same applies to all sorts of other items on loan. Moderation is the key, and be ready to take the item home again if it isn't needed. As a patient, I was desperately anxious not to upset well-wishers.

Pain

I shall not attempt to add to all that has been written on this aspect of terminal illness except to draw the attention of my medical colleagues to the fact that only rarely does pain start suddenly. There is a gradual increase of discomfort spreading out to involve more and more of the body and one's pain threshold rises with it. This presents the problem, in the intermediate stage of terminal illness, of when to call the doctor out. We all have a fear of starting on injections. Generally speaking, I would suggest that if the pain persists for more than two to three hours and has failed to respond to a second dose of analgesics taken one hour after the first, the general practitioner should be informed.

Symptomatic treatment

A further comment to my medical colleagues: please be careful not to overdo the symptomatic treatment. A terminally ill patient will tell you only a fraction of his problems and does not want pills for everything. You will be the one person who can share his physical distress, but do not assume that each symptom has to be treated.

Personal adjustments

These are a gradual process, but a very profound one. The first adjustment concerns the physical aspect of marriage. Intercourse will become more tiring and then the desire for it will disappear. This can be very distressing for the partner where the patient is relatively young. It becomes very difficult to express love for one's spouse as one becomes emotionally drained. While it is reassuring to say, 'I love you,' it becomes more difficult to mean it when the 'love compartment' of one's emotional store becomes swamped with the sheer effort needed to get through the day's limited activities. I suppose the 'feeling' of love changes as bodily distress increases.

The isolation, particularly of the wife where the husband is ill, may be made the worse by his strange hypersensitivity to touch, even from those he loves. I thought I was alone in this, but was told by a nurse experienced in terminal care that patients often long to be left alone. Bed-making, washing and so forth can be acutely distressing. For myself, this hypersensitivity may have been exaggerated by a depressed view of my 'body image', since I was covered in subcutaneous walnut-sized lumps, but the same will apply to a person with a colostomy or mastectomy.

Those who normally share a double bed, will usually have to abandon the practice. This is a personal matter, but it is important that both partners get as much rest as possible.

From these observations, it may be seen that considerable demands are made on the spouse; all those involved with the family should be made aware of this.

Finally, again sharing my own experience, there has to be an adjustment of roles within the family, particularly where the male partner is ill and he has been more dominant in decision-making. Arguments can easily arise, and trying to involve the husband may produce an outburst of frustration because he is unable to carry out his normal role. This increasing helplessness and dependence is more difficult for some people to accept than others. I found it very difficult.

Telling younger members of the family

Not only from our own experience, but also from that of others, I believe it is right that children should be told when a parent has a terminal illness. If it is malignant, the word 'cancer' can perhaps be used, as it does have some meaning for a child, but not the fear and foreboding it arouses in adults. In a Christian home, the subject of death can more positively be spoken of than where life after death has no meaning. The age of the child is important and this creates problems when there is a wide age-range in the family. Even in a normally-spaced family with children ranging from eleven to six years old for example, the reactions of the older children will be very different from those of the younger. However, it is better if the news is shared together, rather than passed from child to child. Certainly one must always be truthful.

When the patient himself is unaware of the diagnosis, or even the seriousness of the condition, the children obviously cannot be told any more than the patient himself. Two books on the subject are recommended:

What's happened to Auntie Jean? A Scripture Union publication.

A death in the family. A Lion publication.

I personally found it difficult to avoid casting a generalised gloom over the household as far as the children were concerned. It was too difficult to laugh and joke over meals, or during a car journey when I was in discomfort. My wife felt I was over-sensitive on this point, but I could not help getting depressed about it. We discreetly arranged long weekends for the children to stay with uncles and aunts or grandparents, and, where applicable, godparents or close friends. These trips were a great success and gave my wife and me more time alone. The children were unaware of our side of the story as the invitation came directly from the various relatives concerned.

The will to survive

As one grows weaker, shorter of breath, distended and uncomfortable, so living becomes more and more of an effort. It is hard not to grow selfish when the simplest matters become like a preparation for a twenty-mile hill-walk. Emotions are squeezed out leaving one feeling like an empty toothpaste tube. There are no reserves left.

Against this background, all but the greatest saints will become moody and irritable, making unkind or hurtful remarks to those they love most. Does he or she really understand what you, the patient, are actually going through? Possibly not, for it is certainly worse than I expected, and I have looked after many patients through terminal illness. But speaking as a patient to a fellow-patient, remember that your loved-one is suffering as acutely as you are but in a different way, and following a path as lonely and desolate as your own.

How much should a doctor tell his patient?

It is an interesting corollary to the old question of how much should a doctor tell his patient about his condition, that a sick doctor will inevitably know the full story. Knowing the very poor prognosis of my own condition has made it more difficult to accept and, because of this, I am moving back to a middle-of-the-road position. A patient's questions must always be answered truthfully, but it is equally important to maintain a note of optimism even against all statistical odds. In spite of improved awareness by the public that 'cancer' is often curable, it is still a death warrant in most people's minds and the word may need to be avoided until the fatal outcome of the condition becomes more certain.

Planning ahead

Some families like to look ahead and plan activities, whereas others will act on impulse, deciding on Saturday morning to have a weekend down on the coast. We belong to the first group and found it hard to have a continuing uncertainty over our heads as to whether or

not I should be well enough to participate, say, in a visit
to see someone or, more particularly, in planning the
summer holiday. In practice, it was easier to assume that
I would not be fit and to make adjustments at the last
minute if I were able to join the family.

*Some special difficulties for the Christian in facing ter-
minal illness:*

1. Without wishing to generalise too much, I think that
there is often a strange unwillingness to be helped. Why?
I suppose we believe that God wants to use our weakness
to demonstrate his power. This becomes a spiritual conflict as much as a physical one and the devil will seek to
misdirect our desire to be independent.

2. There may be disappointment, even resentment,
that one is as much subject to stress symptoms as an
ordinary person. This is particularly true in the early
stages of the condition. Subsequently, inner peace of
mind will reduce the distress of dreams, sleeplessness,
hyperacidity, bowel disturbance, wind, palpitations and
so on. Such was my experience.

3. Introspection can be a very powerful force used by
the devil to upset and disturb Christians. Not only are
past sins constantly brought to mind, but an over-pre-
occupation with our worthlessness in the sight of God
adds to our guilt. Never can God's forgiveness be more
confidently claimed than when we are 'sharing in the
fellowship of Christ's sufferings' (Philippians 3:10).

4. Well-meaning Christian friends will be even more
concerned to share their latest 'good book', cassette
tapes, prayer guide-lines and so on. The problem is compounded because the lender will be confident that his or
her book is just the one for your particular need. Certainly I have appreciated the many books I have been
lent, but again moderation is the key. If you wish to
share something, let me say that I found that I valued the

reading of a psalm together as much as anything else.

5. Loss of faith is a tragic response to suffering and in particular to terminal illness. In some cases, the cause will be that our spiritual house is being built on sand rather than rock (Matthew 7:24–27). It is never too late in life to start rebuilding. In others, the foundations may be secure but the building is of wood, hay and stubble. When challenged by the experience of suffering, we may be forced to realise the shortfall in our lives. It is never too late to rebuild with stone—giving value to the spiritual rather than the material (1 Corinthians 3:11–15). For some others, loss of faith will be apparent rather than real, for the devil will seek to destroy the most precious possession we have. The only answer here is the biblical assurance that God will not let us go. Sometimes I feel that I am holding by my hands to a cliff edge—but even if I let go, it is reassuring to know that I shall not slip down, because I am being held.

For the most part, the experience of suffering and the challenge of terminal illness should be something which will build up our faith and give us great opportunities to share it with others.

Some problems facing a general practitioner:

1. An intimate awareness of the signs of deterioration and an underlying realisation of the possible distressing complications is a very real problem. I can only emphasise that the more painful and distressing cases which come to mind will do so because they are exceptional. As with a mother facing childbirth, the anticipation is usually far more of a problem than the reality.

2. Continuous questions from patients as to one's state of health are well meant but at the end of a morning's surgery to be asked for the twenty-sixth time, 'How are you getting on, Doctor?' is very wearying.

3. The diagnosis eventually has to be made known

among one's patients and it becomes a gossip item for several weeks: 'Is it true that Dr so-and-so has got cancer?' My initial hospital admission was over Christmas, so this presented particular difficulties. As my health deteriorated, I continued to work and was aware of being 'examined' by the patient just as much as I was enquiring and treating his own condition. This experience of 'dying publicly' is probably worse for a general practitioner than for a person in any other occupation. The public exposure of crucifixion to which Christ was subjected was a much-needed source of encouragement to me in this very difficult situation.

4. There is the undoubted problem of knowing when to stop work. Despite all that is said, doctors are usually extremely dedicated and it is possible to continue working against all one's better judgement. It was no coincidence that, the day after my wife and I had prayed over this difficulty, I fell and broke my right arm. It presented an ideal tangible reason for calling it a day, initially with the prospect of returning when it healed, though this later proved to be out of the question.

5. It needs to be said even here, that it is essential to be adequately insured as far as payment for a locum is concerned. All partnerships must insist on this in their contract.

This question of insurance gives me the opportunity to introduce a slightly humorous anecdote, it is so important to keep a sense of humour, however extreme the circumstances.

Just after my first operation, when I was sure I would get better, I was worried because, only two or three months earlier, I had taken out two small insurance policies.

'Why,' I asked, 'if I was going to be healed had God "overruled" in my taking out these policies?' I discussed this with one partner, a committed Calvinist, who is inclined to look on the gloomy side.

'Oh,' he said, 'which company did you insure with?' I told him.

'That's all right,' he said. 'I'm insured with another one!' The senior partner, more of the Arminian persuasion and generally optimistic, on being presented with my dilemma replied, 'I shouldn't worry, James, we are all worth more dead than alive.' I drew little solace from either reply, but had to laugh at both. It was however a houseman, a sincere Catholic, who gave me the answer I needed.

'Well James,' he said, 'just think what you would feel like now if you hadn't got those two policies.'

As it turns out, I have not got better. For my wife's sake, I am grateful that I did take some precaution to provide for her; but even if I hadn't, I know God would have stepped in, in another way. This is in no way meant to influence your attitude to life insurance as normally understood, but there is another yet more secure premium-free life insurance, indeed life certainty. This I have claimed through committing my life to Christ, and this provides the substance and the certainty of my Christian hope.

The Christian Hope

From what has been written so far, I trust it will be obvious that there is nothing special about me as a physical person. I do not believe Christians are spared the physical distress of dying. Why should they be? Having watched others die and their families cope with illness more prolonged than my own, I sometimes feel I am a relative failure. Yet in spite of this, I have been able to perceive a theme of triumph and of victory in my suffering. There is something which has made me valuable, not only to my fellows, but also to the God who made me and who is infinitely concerned that any circumstances I have to face can be used as a means of blessing, and, more importantly, of bringing praise and glory to the Lord Jesus Christ.

'Is this possible?' you may ask.

It is more likely in my particular cancer than in many others—and certainly than in other cases of terminal illness—for the body to become wasted and distorted almost beyond recognition, yet for the spirit, the inner man, the personality, to remain as it was before the illness began. If the spirit can survive such gross mutilation of its 'container', is it not reasonable to suppose it will survive physical death? In terms of the anatomy and physiology of the brain, the arguments are more difficult to follow through. But to you who look on and say, 'I don't get involved in anything like that,' I would reply, 'Change places with me for five minutes and you will realise that one day, without the slightest shadow of doubt, you will be very much involved in something like that.'

What then is the Christian hope, and how has it so radically altered my own attitude to dying as a young man of thirty-seven with a wife and two children whom I am leaving behind?

Hesitantly, but without apology, I must ask you to assume first of all that God is true to his word, and secondly that we find this revealed in the Bible. Without for the moment trying to rationalise it or argue back, look at the promises he has made to those who go through experiences of suffering. (See pages 183–185).

I cannot explain the whys and wherefores of suffering, but with such cast-iron promises as these, there is a secure foundation on which we can start. Even though my 'good' days are so often swallowed up by days of frustration and disappointment, irritation and discomfort, these promises do not alter.

From here I should go on to describe the substance of my hope. Hope here is used in the way St. Paul uses it, as a positive affirmation, rather than trusting to luck. As I did for fine weather on my wedding day.

I believe that there is no ground for fear of death and what comes after. The process of dying is one of which I do sometimes become fearful, and this is a natural reaction and one that was experienced, I believe, even by our Lord himself in Gethsemane. But the freedom from fear of death itself, is even more liberating when it is seen in the biblical context. Forgiveness lies in a personal acceptance of the death of Christ on our behalf, not dying as a man might die for his country or his family, but as the Son of God, for a sinful person: that is, me. Once such a step has been taken, hope begins to take shape; and once the underlying truth of the resurrection has been understood, the real wonder of it all becomes crystal clear. This new life becomes ours; only a shadow now, but after death to go on for ever. The choice is ours. All the facts are available to us. God's judgement will be manifestly fair, most of all to those who are judged. This is not easy to accept, but I can promise each and every one who takes such a step of faith that any fear of death will go.

Dying we live

Strange to relate, however, my life as a practising Christian was changed by the knowledge that I was dying almost more than if I had been a committed atheist. Suddenly all that I had been told or read in the Bible made sense. My lifestyle didn't change very much but my attitude did; it was as if I suddenly started really to live, although the reverse was true, and I was dying. A clear spring morning is most meaningful after weeks of dull wet weather. The slow build-up of dust on a car windscreen goes unnoticed till I clean it with a few squirts of water and the windscreen wipers. So life can really be understood when it is contrasted with death.

This is impossible for a normal healthy person to accept it just doesn't make sense. However, it does help to have much more awareness of life if we think of it as a journey, with a sure destination. Christ spoke clearly of the broad way that leads to destruction and the narrow way that leads to life (Matthew 7:13–14). The idea is put across in that much neglected book *Pilgrim's Progress*. Once the *celestial city* comes into view—to use the analogy from Bunyan's story—life is never quite the same. For me, I suddenly became free, free to live as a person in my own right. I suppose the reaction of a medical friend, on hearing that I had cancer, struck a similar note.

'Well, James, if I were you, I'd really go out and enjoy myself for a year,' he said. But only if I had had complete certainty that death was total destruction could I justify that attitude. You must believe me when I say yet again, that as death gets closer, its finality becomes more difficult really to accept.

What else did this freedom mean? Life itself became more precious. My attitude to requests for termination of pregnancy changed from being rather more liberal to one of almost urgent persuasion to go ahead with the pregnancy. I could do nothing else; nothing else made sense.

My attitude to possessions changed, too. I remember, in particular that when we refitted our kitchen, I started out planning the best—split level this, and microwave that, and so on, involving many hundreds of pounds. But when I realised that I probably wouldn't be here in a year anyway, that the food would taste no different, and that my wife might well move house, we agreed together on something costing less than a quarter of the price we might have paid. To return to the same picture of the journey, we are all moving house and not one item can go with us. This makes life much more exciting, not more dull as the glossy magazines imply.

The final new element of freedom is to look back on life's achievements and really ask what they count for. It is a very sobering exercise. The qualifications, degrees and the like, suddenly become worth no more than the paper on which they are written. It is the contents not the container that really matters. This is familiar ground but it cannot be emphasised enough in these days of 'Christian' materialism.

It might be appropriate to conclude this section with a few comments on that archetypal sufferer in the Old Testament, Job himself. I do not find this story easy, not least because he ended up seven times better off than when he started, while I am in the process of a rather uncomfortable death. But it is also a cautionary tale, directed against slick arguments from writers like myself. We should be careful with 'explanations' of suffering. God judges people harshly if they use ruthless logic. The solution finally revealed by the story, is a vision that Job had of God's greatness and eternal purpose, the celestial city of *Pilgrim's Progress* perhaps, the destination of our journey. Although I am not normally a man of spiritual visions, this was in some measure my experience too, and it has helped me to endure very considerable distress. But such visions are not common.

What I find most difficult about the book of Job is its 'pre-Christian' introduction where Satan is allowed to 'test' Job, then report back to God on how he had fared. At one time, I became bitter against God because I felt he was looking on rather like a torture-supervisor, quietly authorising more and more distressing experiences to see how soon I, the prisoner, would crack. The rack was slowly tightened, the thumbscrew remorselessly turned. Now I reject this picture totally, whatever conservative Biblical scholarship may say. Peace of mind came suddenly when reading *Daily Light* one evening in February—'In all their affliction he was afflicted' (Isaiah 63:9).

The New Testament teaching on suffering takes it into an entirely different sphere. Our Lord is not standing by seeing how we get on; he is actually suffering with us. Our pain is his pain, our swollen useless limbs are his; but, ultimately, our weakness becomes his strength and our defeat becomes his victory. Here lies one more, and surely the most profound, truth about suffering: it enables us to identify most closely with our Lord. Yes, we can wash each other's feet; we can go about doing good; on our good days, we can show certain Christian virtues. The Bible speaks of these, quite bluntly, as 'filthy rags' by contrast with our Lord's perfect life: a rather sobering thought. But in suffering, I believe, we come closest to knowing Christ. Many months before his actual crucifixion, he spoke of his disciples taking up their cross daily and following him; and, I believe, suffering prepares us, in some special way, for our service in heaven. This may be wishful thinking from one who has had to endure a great deal, but I don't think so: I believe it to be true.

Finally, suffering brings unique opportunities for God's name to be glorified, and for people to turn to faith. For everyone who says, 'Well, if God allows that, I'll have nothing to do with him,' there'll be another who will affirm, 'If that man or woman can endure such circumstances, I must see where he gets the strength to do it.' Equally, Christian friends have been much more aware of spiritual reality through watching me die, and their faith and witness has, in many cases, been totally transformed. I don't know why this should be, but they tell me that it is so.

Peace through pain

Pain is an intensely subjective sensation which some people are naturally able to tolerate better than others. It is common experience that if one's mind is occupied in some activity, pain is less distressing. The same is true if, emotionally and spiritually, one is at rest, free from worry. So often, behind the scenes, relatives are working out how much they stand to gain in the will. Others refuse to take their share in caring for the dying because of a long-standing family feud. It might reasonably be supposed that a committed Christian is at a big advantage over those who honestly admit, in their own minds, that they face a completely unknown future (even though relatives and friends may think in terms of their living on in eternal bliss).

But even as far as Christians are concerned, it is sad that many lack the confidence which the New Testament writers unanimously affirm. The doctrine of purgatory lacks biblical support in my view, and both Roman Catholics and Protestants have a lot to answer for in their failure to give clear teaching on the certainty of life hereafter, for those with a trust in Christ and a knowledge of sin forgiven. The reason for this lack of clear teaching is that it throws into a rather embarrassing contrast the destiny of those who do not have such a belief. Certainly, God is a just and perfect judge in these matters; equally certainly, we are not just or right, and judgement to come is clearly spoken of in the Bible.

Assurance is something all true believers should know as they approach death: a deep peace of mind. The Bible speaks of this as 'the anchor of the soul'. Whatever physical buffeting we may experience, and even should we capsize, our ship is unsinkable and that anchor will always hold. Clearer Bible teaching on death and bereavement is desperately needed in our churches today.

Christians respond to suffering in different ways. It might be helpful to illustrate this by quoting a letter and a funeral address. The letter gives a firsthand account of suffering; in the address, the speaker comments on a close friend's response to his own suffering. The people involved may not be typical but some of you may know others with similar experiences and responses.

A LETTER FROM MARY BOSANQUET

A year ago I was operated on for breast cancer. The surgeon told me that there was an eighty per cent chance of recovery. So I took it for granted that I would recover completely. But nine months later, symptoms of the trouble recurred. Now I have been ill for three months. My left arm is crippled, so that I cannot drive the car or ride or work in the house or in the garden. I am often in pain. I rarely sleep through the night. In order to avoid being actually incapacitated by pain, I have to live a quiet life, with regular rest and exercise and not much else.

Small changes in my condition sometimes make my blood run cold with fear, and often my heart aches almost intolerably at the thought of the grief that may lie ahead for the children, and for Robert, my dear husband, to whom I have been married for almost twenty-two years.

All this suffering I share with thousands upon thousands of other people. What I would love to do is to share, too, something of the joy which contains it and the great depths of peace which lie under it, like the life-giving waters that lie hidden under the fields and woods. I am proving the truth of what Christ said to his followers, 'My own peace I give you.' This is because God in Christ has revealed himself to me in a new way, and his presence has become increasingly real to me in this suffering.

Although I have for many years known something of what it means to offer my life to Christ and practise the realisation of his presence. I have recently, in a new way, been able to see his glory everywhere, to know him better and to be more ready to accept his will. I know that when he said, 'Happy are those who mourn, God will comfort them,' he meant exactly that. And the word translated as 'comfort' does not mean 'make comfortable' but 'make strong'. What makes us strong in his presence, a presence which is here with us now and also waiting for us on the other side of death, 'an anchor for our lives, an anchor safe and sure. It enters in through the veil, where Jesus has entered on our behalf as fore-runner'.

This joy which I am experiencing in spite of my suffering, is shared by my husband. It clothes all our grief and our anxiety in light and overflows to the children, so that often the house is full of laughter and everything around us flowers into life. The reason is quite simple: through the very intensity of what we are suffering, the reality of God's love has blazed up in our lives, transfiguring everything.

I must go back to my own individual experience because ultimately, and especially in suffering, every one of us is alone with God. Yet in this very aloneness I feel myself supported not only by the love of my dear family and my many friends, but also, and this is vital, by their prayers.

Meanwhile there is plenty of living still to be done on this side. My life is changed but it is not ended. Although I cannot do anything practical for people, now I can live for them more than ever. I can live to share this joy with them and to love them, to empty myself of all the ob-structive remains of *me*, so that I am just a river-bed through which God's own love can flow out and speak to their hearts.

'If anyone wants to come with me, he must forget himself, carry his cross and follow me.' When Jesus says that, he is asking for everything, our whole selves, emptied like this, so that he can live in us.

To me now, taking up my cross daily means a perfectly concrete thing. It means daily discipline, schooling myself to patience. It means leaving behind willingly a life of perfect health and almost inexhaustible energy, in which I rode on horseback across Canada, travelled all over Italy with the British Army, married and bore three children, and wrote six books, and all with strength to spare.

Now I must learn to be quite a different person, content to have no strength of my own any longer, but only the strength that God gives me from day to day. I, who trained my body to be fit and my mind to be active, must now train myself to bear pain without betraying it in my face or voice, and to keep the anxiety to myself and only share the joy. And as I learn to give up my whole life into God's hands, I must remember that it *is* in his hands and that he can give it back to me if he will, to live and serve him here for many years yet.

Yes, it means patience and discipline continually renewed. But the strength to continue in it is inexhaustible just because it is not my own, but the strength of Jesus— Jesus who has said: 'I and my Father are one,' and in whom all the love and the power of God are concentrated, as the sunlight is concentrated in a burning-glass.

This is what I would love to share with a few of the thousands who are suffering as I am—and more than I am. So take this and use it however you can.

Yours in the love of Jesus,

MARY.

PART OF THE ADDRESS GIVEN BY RODNEY SCHOFIELD
AT THE FUNERAL OF
THE REVEREND BENJAMIN TURNOCK

C. S. Lewis wrote of the poet and critic Charles Williams, 'No event has so corroborated my faith in the next world as Williams did simply in dying. When the idea of death and the idea of Williams thus met in my mind, it was the idea of death which changed.' So, speaking on behalf of those who saw him in the last twelve months, it also was with Ben. By the way he died, he changed our idea of death. It's not, I think, necessary today to dwell on his life and his works: they'll be taken up in the memorial service at Trull. But I do want to share with you the immense privilege of having seen him die. It's not easy to describe it as clearly or as carefully as one would wish, but I'd say that for me, in one sense, Ben died not last week but somewhere round about Christmas time. That's to say, it was then that he became rather cut off from us in the normal way. Communication about everyday affairs became limited. He was able sometimes to appreciate our conversation, but his own contribution was reduced to the occasional whisper. And yet, in another and more important way, he wasn't cut off from us at all. He was able to share and transmit something very much more wonderful in quite a different way. In his body he was frequently twisted with pain and underwent suffering which was very distressing to watch, yet in himself he was entering a realm of which I doubt many of us here have much knowledge at all. His face was lit with joy; his concern was to let us know that we needn't fear or grieve because, as he said several times, 'The dear Lord is calling me home; it's going to be wonderful.'

It's as if he could already see for himself the heavenly places, and as if their light and their beauty were reflected in his face. He said to me on one occasion, 'The sunshine' and I thought at first he was talking about the weather, because it had been raining earlier. But no, I was mistaken: he was talking about the sunshine he could see inside him. Having been with Ben this last month, there is a passage—a climactic passage—in *The Pilgrim's Progress* which at last has come alive for me, and speaks of something real. I want to read you just a few sentences from it.

'And now were these men, as it were, *in* heaven, before they came at it, being swallowed up with the sight of angels, and with hearing of their melodious notes. Here also they had the city itself in view, and they thought they heard all the bells therein to ring, to welcome them thereto. But above all, the warm and joyful thoughts that they had about their own dwelling there, with such company, and that for ever and ever. Oh, by what tongue or pen can their glorious joy be expressed! *And thus they came up to the gate.*'

If there is any addition one would want to make to that description, it's that the vision of God is never something that one can keep to oneself. Ben was in the presence, and it was impossible not to know it. Love shone in his face, and embraced all of us as well.

That death will remain with me as a great witness to the faith. It's all true. It's a reality. The Lord is risen indeed, and hath appeared (as it says) to Simon—yes, but to Ben also, and to countless other faithful disciples who have now entered into the joy of their Lord.

By way of contrast, and perhaps by way of slight encouragement to others, my own experiences have been very different. I have very little joy to clothe my grief and anxiety in light and it is almost all minor complaints which my dear wife and children have to put up with. I simply do not have the strength or emotional resources to 'bear pain without betraying it in my face or voice, and to keep the anxiety to myself and only share the joy'. But God does give grace even in my great weakness. Instead of joy, I frequently find I am crying out in anger and frustration to God, as to what is being achieved by the sheer hell I seem to be going through.

'Who can possibly be benefiting?' I ask him. 'Why me, just an ordinary weak person?' The answer can only lie in this very fact of my weakness bringing greater glory and honour to God, in a way we cannot now understand but shall, in the life hereafter. Also I suspect that my own condition is considerably more advanced, and therefore more distressing.

Initially, I felt a great sense of personal failure when I read Mary's letter and discussed it with my wife and several friends. We agreed that for the majority, it is much better to say when we are in pain, particularly to those who are closest to us. Then we all know where we stand. Indeed, I often make a point, having shared all the good things God has done, of saying exactly how very distressing the whole experience is from a physical point of view. I am not embarrassed if I end up in tears, as it gives me great emotional release and does make it easier to bear.

Finally, I take great solace from our Lord's experience of suffering on the cross. Certainly, the 'joy' spoken of was 'the joy that was set before him': that is, the future joy of glory in heaven. He too felt isolated and 'let down' by God at his hour of greatest need as he cried out, 'My God, why hast thou forsaken me?'

Why me?

Although I have left it till now, this question is the first one we ask when, suddenly, that illness or accident which up to now has always happened only to others, happens to me. When the news of cancer is broken by a surgeon or a GP, it is normal to reject it outright or, if not, to assume that the condition can be cured. Fortunately, this is frequently true; also even if the statistical odds are against such a possibility, people tend to reject them and go on hoping. So people hope that they will be cured and some are cured. But I want to speak to those who, like me, find evidence that something else is wrong, weeks or months after the treatment and 'cure'.

For, the moment of such a discovery moved me from an area of experience which I knew and could control, into the great unknown; into a cruel, new world, where I was on my own—or so it seemed.

I was dying. I kept waking up in the night, supposing that I had been having a bad dream, but a quick feel of my armpit confirmed that the lump was there. I was trapped like an animal in a cage. Whatever other sentiments I may have expressed in this book, whatever gentle rebukes or amusing asides, let it not be underestimated that the experience was totally appalling. There were brief moments when I could forget it: at a Christmas party, on a seaside beach, or when making love, but then I would be brought back to reality— 'James, you are dying from cancer.' Never in my professional career had I realised what a burden this diagnosis, in particular, places on a person. The effect was total.

Unlike what happens when sudden fatal accidents occur, one has time to think, time to adjust; but still the question comes back, 'Why me?'

It was only as I had to spend time in hospital—mornings in outpatient clinics or, worse still, two floors underground waiting for radiotherapy—that the question came the other way round, 'Why *not* me?' Although I have spent my life seeing sick people, or people who thought they were sick, it still came as a shock to draw aside the screen we each put around ourselves and see the sheer numbers of those who are involved in illness of one kind or another. I saw more clearly than before that disease is part of our human condition, originating, according to the Bible which I, as a Christian believe, with the rejection of God's order.

It is not a question of fairness or unfairness, certainly not on God's part; nor does the phrase so often used, 'It doesn't seem right,' make sense. Of course it is not *right,* but watch a few television documentaries from overseas and it is clear that there is very little 'right' in the world at all. Or, nearer home, look at the frequent demonstrations, the problem of unemployment, housing shortages and broken marriages.

The Christian answer is to turn again to God's promise, that God cares, that he loves and that no situation is beyond solution—and the solution will not be a compromise; rather, good will be created from the wreckage.

This is all grossly oversimplified. I must admit there are certain special problems for the Christian when we start looking futher at God's promises referred to previously (e.g. 'Whatsoever you ask in my name, that I will do'). However, if God is in control of our lives, it is to be expected that he can use 'suffering', just as much as a superb family holiday or a mountain walk, to show us more of his purpose. Without being blasphemous, I believe that even God Almighty cannot rid the world of suffering until the return of Christ at the Second Coming. It is just impossible, any other way. Instead, he uses it; used it most supremely when Jesus Christ came into the world, identified himself totally with our human state and suffered through to death itself. Unlike human suffering in general, this was a direct consequence of man's rejection of and rebellion against God.

Since it is no longer a punishment for wrong-doing, the experience of suffering takes on a new meaning for a Christian. Sometimes it is used to enrich our Christian experience, or to bring people to faith. It is uncommon, but for the one concerned it will be unmistakable, that God permits suffering as a means of correction. Heating metal can get it straight. Refining a precious metal cleanses it. This was indeed how God spoke to me. A small seed planted in a poorly disciplined area of my life years earlier grew to such proportions that I lost all control of it. It was literally a soul-destroying process but needed simple action on my part to eradicate it. This I had repeatedly refused to do, although it had penetrated almost every part of my thought processes. Eventually God dealt with it in his own radical way—my cancer was confirmed; I took the necessary action that very day and emerged a free man.

To begin with, I was sure I was cured, but it proved not to be the case. This was very hard to accept, but it all depends on how clear our vision is of eternity—the celestial city I spoke of. Once this world is seen as a time of preparation, a transit flight, a train journey, then, when I am prepared and God's purpose has been achieved, what is wrong in being shown a short-cut to the summit? Steep it may be, but, like the north face of the Eiger, I believe there is a special reward for those who are chosen for such a route.

Before leaving this section, I would caution my medical colleagues in particular about these small seeds that can so quickly choke spiritual life. They include overriding ambition, a large private practice, the yacht on the South Coast, too lavish entertainment and—dare I mention it—alcohol. But every man must work out the implications for himself.

Endurance and despair

Endurance is not a popular concept these days. Just as car light bulbs and washing machines are designed to need replacement with unfailing regularity, so the idea of sticking to a job and seeing something through, like life-long marriage or honouring a contract in specified terms, is now seen, by some, as an old-fashioned attitude. But endurance is high in the list of Christian virtues, as it affects both our secular and spiritual lives.

Suffering and terminal illness do sometimes bring out remarkable qualities of endurance in people in whom one would least expect it; both in patients and in those who are involved in their care.

Christians face particular problems here, because they often suppose that God should intervene earlier than he does or in a different way. I can only direct my thoughts back to the unchangeable promises of God, and to the certainty that he is a hair's breadth away from me in the physical aspects of my suffering and has a purpose through each and every incident.

Practically speaking, we must keep communications open between him and us. Our Bible reading should be short and simple, but it is important to read the Bible rather than a 'blessed thought' by even the most inspired expositor. Radio services have been an enormous source of strength to me but, as long as possible, it is a good mental and spiritual discipline to attend a place of worship. In those denominations where it is traditional to move to another part of the church to receive Communion (e.g. Anglican), do not be too proud to ask the minister to bring it down to you, wherever you can remain seated.

Finally, the morning and evening verses collected in the *Daily Light* under each day of the year have been a means of blessing to many hundreds and are a restful way to close the day.

At an appropriate moment, it is very helpful to share the hymns and readings you would like at the funeral. Do not dwell on this too long as it can make you and the family too introspective, but when the moment comes, it is wonderful for the mourners to feel that this is what you especially wanted and chose with them.

The other word used to head this paragraph is 'despair', and one might add the word 'guilt'. As I mentioned earlier, how important it is not to dwell on the past, supposing that God is punishing us, for some sinful action. Look back, rather, on all the good things, and look around for opportunities to witness to him wherever you are. Such thoughts of guilt are entirely inspired by the Devil who, we read in the book of Revelation, chapter 12, verse 10, is the 'accuser of our brethren'.

Saying 'goodbye' to guests can be difficult as one approaches the end. I was much helped by someone who spoke of a friend in the same position as myself who said goodbye to his visitors with the words, 'See you here or there,' pausing as the meaning of the phrase sank in. Said with understanding it is the Christian 'au revoir'. In marked contrast—and this filled me with sorrow—was the parting remark from another friend, a life-long church-goer' 'Good luck, James.' I wonder which phrase would really express your feelings?

What are my feelings as I write these final paragraphs? Firstly, surprise that I have survived long enough to finish this. Some days I have felt so ill that it seemed I could not possibly awake the next morning. Secondly, a conviction that even if one person benefits through it, the effort will have been worthwhile. Thirdly, the unceasing awareness of the spiritual world as my body weakens, of music on the distant hill becoming louder, of the vision of glory becoming more clear now that my journey is almost over.

Divine healing

This poses a difficult problem. I should like to direct this section to Christian doctors and members of Christian

Medical Fellowship in particular. While it is admirable to organise symposia on ethics at BMA House, we are still frightened to grasp this particular nettle of healing. Try spending a day—no, rather a week or a month—as I have done, looking out from a living room couch on clear sunny days to watch the rest of the family active in the garden whilst I feel too tired or ill to move. Alternatively, come to know the penetrating discomfort of nerve root pain, which is totally unrelieved by rubbing, changes of position, local heat and normal pain-killers.

Have we not as Christian doctors more to offer? Is it really sufficient to arrive next morning, white-coated or smooth-suited, to enquire patiently about bowels, bladder and appetite, to request from the relatives yet more tender loving care or, even, to promise to pray. I believe that Christian gospel goes further than this, and I am speaking as one whose assurance of salvation is total, whose awareness of the Saviour's loving care for me is absolute. For some, God has a purpose of divine healing even against natural law. The problem is how to search for this.

We need constantly to re-examine our approach and put off the armour-plating which shields us from honesty on this issue. Some discountenance divine healing altogether but, on behalf of those of us who are patients, I urge them to think again, and I believe there will be rich blessing through an open attitude. My plea is for fresh thinking on this issue! But from my own experience, I would warn against the following dangers:

1. That people, including committed Christians, have so much 'faith' that they presume they will be healed. The balance between genuine expectant faith and wishful thinking is almost impossible to achieve.

2. That faith will be undermined rather than built up if God's answer is 'No'.

3. That the sick person will search endlessly for the

past sin to be forgiven so that healing will finally occur. Such thinking is unbiblical, but so easily creeps in.

4. That a measure of mental gymnastics is required to believe God can and will heal, while knowing, in more logical moments that the chances are that he will not.

5. That a quiet, steady adjustment to terminal illness can be disturbed by the introduction of uncertainty almost amounting to insecurity through the question: 'I wonder if I shall be healed?'

6. That increased introspection—'Are the lumps bigger or smaller? Is this symptom better or worse?'—can completely ruin an otherwise reasonably comfortable day.

7. That the sick person will be even more exposed to direct or indirect enquiries from those praying for him, all with enormous 'faith', each looking for an answer to their particular prayer: 'Is the pain in your leg better?' etc. If the answer is 'worse', the person feels very deflated and 'fellowship' is difficult to continue.

More could be said but these were issues I personally encountered to a greater or lesser extent. There was no doubt that 'healing' took place for me at an emotional level during a time when I was very depressed about my condition. Furthermore, in spite of what I have said above, there were specific answers to prayer about a number of most distressing symptoms. In particular I was relieved of nausea and vomiting which I am sure was psychosomatic in origin.

However, the conflict of whether I was doing everything correctly did trouble me. Release came with the realisation that the whole issue was out of my hands. One morning I had a clear picture that I was in a boat. Before, when asking for healing, it was as though I had been in a punt where one stands at one end pushing on the punt pole and steering more or less expertly. But now, I was in a rowing boat, my back to the direction in which I was going, but travelling in a much more leisurely fashion. The great joy was that the Lord was at the tiller, his face gently smiling and his eyes twinkling as he quietly guided me to my destination.

Was I healed? Yes I believe I was.

Bible promises on the steadfast love of God

Numbers 24 v. 19. God is not man that he should lie, or a son of man that he should change his mind. Has he said and will he not do it? Or has he spoken and will he not fulfil it?

Hebrews 6 v. 18, 19. God . . . interposed with an oath, so that . . . we . . . might have strong encouragement to seize the hope set before us. We have this as a sure and steadfast anchor of the soul.

Proverbs 3 v. 24. If you sit down you will not be afraid; when you lie down your sleep will be sweet.

Psalm 4 v. 8. In peace I will both lie down and sleep; for thou alone, O Lord, makest me dwell in safety.

2 Corinthians 1 v. 3–5. Blessed be the God and Father of our Lord Jesus Christ, the Father of all mercies and God of all comfort, who comforts us all in our affliction, so that we may be able to comfort those who are in any affliction, with the comfort with which we ourselves are comforted by God. For as we share abundantly in Christ's sufferings, so through Christ we share abundantly in comfort too.

Deuteronomy 31 v. 8. It is the Lord who goes before you; he will be with you, he will not fail or forsake you; do not fear or be dismayed.

Hebrews 5 v. 8, 9. [Jesus] learned obedience through what he suffered; and being made perfect he became the source of eternal salvation to all who obey him.

John 14 v. 2, 3. In my Father's house are many rooms; If it were not so, would I have told you that I go to prepare a place for you?

Revelation 7 v. 15–17. He who sits upon the throne will shelter them with his presence. They shall hunger no more, neither thirst any more; the sun shall not strike them, nor any scorching heat. For the Lamb in the midst of the throne will be their shepherd, and he will guide them to springs of living water; and God will wipe away every tear from their eyes.

Revelation 21 v. 4. He will wipe every tear from their eyes, and death shall be no more, neither shall there be mourning nor crying nor pain any more, for the former things have passed away.

Psalm 48 v. 14. This is God, our God for ever and ever. He will be our guide for ever.

Psalm 73 v. 23–24. I am continually with thee; thou dost hold my right hand. Thou dost guide me with thy counsel, and afterward thou wilt receive me to glory.

Acts 20 v. 24. I do not account my life of any value nor as precious to myself, if only I may accomplish my course and the ministry which I received from the Lord Jesus, to testify to the gospel of the grace of God.

Isaiah 26 v. 3. Thou dost keep him in perfect peace, whose mind is stayed on thee, because he trusts in thee.

1 Peter 4 v. 12, 13. Do not be surprised at the fiery ordeal which comes upon you to prove you, as though something strange were happening to you. But rejoice in so far as you share Christ's sufferings, that you may also rejoice and be glad when his glory is revealed.

1 Peter 5 v. 7. Cast all your anxieties on him for he cares about you.

2 Corinthians 12 v. 9, 10. The Lord . . . said to me, 'My grace is sufficient for you, for my power is made perfect in weakness.' I will all the more gladly boast of my weaknesses, that the power of Christ may rest upon me.

2 Corinthians 4 v. 16, 17. So we do not lose heart. Though our outer nature is wasting away, our inner

nature is being renewed every day. For this slight momentary affliction is preparing us for an eternal weight of glory beyond comparison.

Isaiah 43 v. 1, 2. Thus says the Lord, he who created you . . . he who formed you . . : 'Fear not, for I have redeemed you; I have called you by name, you are mine. When you pass through the waters I will be with you; and through the rivers, they shall not overwhelm you.'

Psalm 91 v. 1, 2. He who dwells in the shelter of the Most High, who abides in the shadow of the Almighty, will say to the Lord, 'My refuge and my fortress; my God in whom I trust.'

Psalm 41 v. 3. The Lord sustains him on his sick-bed; in his illness thou healest all his infirmities.

Psalm 36 v. 5, 6. Thy steadfast love, O Lord, extends to the heavens, thy faithfulness to the clouds. Thy righteousness is like the mountains of God, thy judgments are like the great deep; man and beast thou savest, O Lord.

Isaiah 63 v. 9. In all their affliction he was afflicted, and the angel of his presence saved them; in his love and in his pity he redeemed them; he lifted them up and carried them all the days of old.

Psalm 55 v. 22. Cast your burden on the Lord, and he will sustain you.

John 13 v. 7. What I am doing you do not know now, but afterward you will understand.

(Quoted from the *Revised Standard Version*.)

DYING

—

**THE GREATEST
ADVENTURE
OF MY LIFE**

James H. Casson

The chapter reproduced in this book is
published as a booklet, and is available from:—

The Christian Medical Fellowship
157 Waterloo Road
London SE1 8XN

Price for a single copy 60p (plus 20p p & p)